DATE DUE		

FASTER THAN A HORSE
Moving West with Engine Power

WESTMINSTER PRESS BOOKS
BY
SUZANNE HILTON

Faster Than a Horse
Moving West with Engine Power

We the People
The Way We Were 1783–1793

Getting There
Frontier Travel Without Power

Here Today and Gone Tomorrow
The Story of World's Fairs and Expositions

Who Do You Think You Are?
Digging for Your Family Roots

The Way It Was—1876

It's Smart to Use a Dummy

FASTER THAN A HORSE

Moving West with Engine Power

by

SUZANNE HILTON

THE WESTMINSTER PRESS 1983
Philadelphia

First edition

Published by The Westminster Press ®
Philadelphia, Pennsylvania

PRINTED IN THE UNITED STATES OF AMERICA
9 8 7 6 5 4 3 2 1

Library of Congress Cataloging in Publication Data

Hilton, Suzanne.
Faster than a horse.

Bibliography: p.
Includes index.
SUMMARY: Describes what it was like to travel by steamboat, steam locomotive, trolley car, and automobile when these inventions were still very new. Lists places across the country where the reader can ride in antique conveyances.
1. Transportation—United States—History—Juvenile literature. 2. United States—Description and travel—Juvenile literature. [1. Transportation—History]
I. Title.
HE203.H479 1983 380.5′0973 83-17022
ISBN 0-664-32709-5

Contents

Faster . . . Faster!

No other country in the modern world was settled in the same way as the United States. Almost every day its frontier moved a little farther west.

After the Louisiana Purchase in 1803 almost doubled the size of the country, people began to wonder how they would ever settle the West when it was so far away. Certainly the ordinary horse was not the answer. A settler who wanted to reach the frontier—which in 1803 was about two thousand miles from the East Coast—could see that his food, his family's health, and good traveling weather would run out long before he reached his destination. There had to be some way to move faster.

This is the story about some of the inventions that eventually tied a great sprawling country together, and about the people whose lives they affected. Never was one of these new discoveries greeted with an encouraging remark like, "Ah-h-h, *that's* just what we need!"

"When I was building my first boat, the *Clermont*, at New York," said Robert Fulton, "I often loitered unknown near the idle group of strangers, gathered in little circles, and heard various inquiries about the object of this new vehicle. Their language was that of scorn, sneer, or ridicule . . . and endless repetition of 'Fulton's Folly'. . . . Never did a bright hope or warm wish cross my path."

But this book is not about the inventors who struggled alone to solve some of America's transportation problems. Many books have already been written about the *history* of steamboats, railroads, trolley cars, and automobiles. This book is about the travelers who went west in them before they were "finished"—if any invention can be said to be finished. Had it not been for these first patient passengers, the sometimes clumsy and often uncomfortable inventions might have been given up as useless visions of crazy inventors.

1
Steamboating on the River

Good-night, Joe.
Goodnight, Flo,—
Don't forget now, dear.
  Next Sunday at two,
  I'll be waiting for you
On the old iron pier.
 —"On a Sunday Afternoon"
Words by Andrew B. Sterling

Crazy John Fitch's Craft

"We reigned Lord high admirals of the Delaware," said John Fitch to anyone who would listen on April 16, 1790. "No Boat on the River could hold way with us, but all fell a-stern, altho several Sail Boats which were very light, and with heavy sails that brought their Gunwails well down to the water, came to try us.

"We also passed many Boats with Oars, which were strong manned, and with no loading, who seemed almost to stand still when we passed them. We also ran Round a Vessel that was beating to windward in about two miles, which had about 1½ miles a start of us. And we came in without any of our works failing."

Fitch decided that morning that perhaps his long list of troubles had come to an end. At last he allowed himself to dream ahead—to the Ohio and Mississippi rivers. His "steamboat" would have to move twice as fast on the Delaware River if he wanted to compete with the stagecoaches that carried passengers from Philadelphia to Trenton. This boat, though, was fast enough for the Ohio River where the stagecoach competition was bogged down in mud and unfinished roads.

But Fitch's problems were not over. He could not get enough money to build his steam-boat in Pittsburgh at the head of the Ohio River. He decided to try raising the money himself by running his boat regularly up the Delaware River and occasionally taking day trips downstream. He built a small cabin to protect passengers in bad weather and set the fare at a low five shillings (one dollar) between Philadelphia and Trenton. The price beat his horse-drawn competitors, and certainly the comfort would. Now if he could only convince travelers that the waterway was nicer than the roadway.

John Fitch's steamboat, the first to carry passengers upstream, had rows of paddles on each side

"The Steam-Boat," read the advertisement he inserted in a Philadelphia newspaper on June 14, "is now ready to take Passengers and is intended to set off from Arch Street Ferry in Philadelphia every Monday, Wednesday, and Friday."

"That crazy Little Johnny Fitch!" said many readers that day, using the name that most people called him behind his back.

What surprised them most was that Fitch claimed his steam-boat would leave the wharf one day and return the next. For four years now they had watched his steam boiler boat constantly getting out of order. Besides, everyone who had ever sailed on a ship knew that captains were famed for announcing departure dates and leaving one, two, three days later. At best, sailing ships left a wharf on the announced day and then anchored out in the river, waiting hours for the tide and wind to change. Water travel had always been that way. No one could imagine anything different.

Another surprise awaited passengers who arrived at the Arch Street Ferry dock after the hour announced for departure. The boat was not there.

"Can you row us out to it then?" the shocked passengers asked young men around the dock who owned rowing skiffs.

But Fitch's steam-boat was far up the river, moving faster than any known boat could possibly follow against the current. In all of history, no one had heard of a boat leaving at the announced hour without at least waiting for late arrivals.

Fitch's sixty-foot-long boat was the first passenger steamboat to carry travelers upstream to other towns. He kept to his schedule during the week as well as he could between machinery breakdowns. On Sundays he searched for important visitors to impress with his steam-boat. When members of Congress were not meeting in Congress Hall, Fitch often persuaded a few to take a ride. One Sunday he took out a number of Indians, with General Mifflin, and McGillivray, the famous Indian trader. But no matter how hard Fitch tried, the people were not ready for his steam-boat.

Travelers continued to take passage in sailing ships that were slowed down by the wind and current, and in stage-coaches that sank to the wheel hubs in mud and bounced wildly over rocky roads. For the next fifteen years many inventors built steamboats and tried them out on lakes and rivers. Fitch's boat was not the first or the last.

Robert Fulton carried a boatload of passengers on his *Clermont* from New York City to Albany in 1806 in just thirty-two hours. The roads were so bad that Fulton knew he had beaten his horse-drawn competitor by a day or two. He was so happy over this success that he managed to get a monopoly on using the entire Hudson River just for his own steamboats. When a few other inventors tried running their boats on the Hudson, Fulton called in the law. The rival steamboats were usually turned over to him and were chopped up in Fulton's yard.

John Fitch was dead long before the seed he tried to plant finally took root. The people he tried to talk into traveling by steamboat just didn't think they needed a steamboat. In the years ahead, though, people began to wonder whether it wasn't a good idea.

Flatboatmen rode down the Ohio and Mississippi rivers in six weeks. Then they either had to find their way back north on foot or spend the next five months pulling their boats against the current. Ship passengers often complained of ending a miserable six- to eight-week voyage from Europe, only to be greeted at the entrance to New York harbor by winds so strong that they had to sail back and forth for days before they could pass the Narrows. Stagecoach and horseback travelers dreamed of moving faster—people like Jacob Harvey, who planned a six-week trip to a small village in Ohio. His trip actually took thirteen weeks—twice the expected time.

Very few Americans thought that a machine like Fitch's "teakettle on a raft" was the way to go. But Fitch had planted the idea and shown that steamboats could work.

The Roosevelts' Fire Canoe

Lydia Latrobe, seventeen, had fallen in love with Nicholas Roosevelt, age forty-one, and married him over her father's objections on November 15, 1808. Nicholas had fallen head over heels in love with steamboats. When he told Lydia that he would like to go down the Ohio and Mississippi rivers in a flatboat the next spring, and do it all over again the following year in a steamboat, Lydia was a little surprised. She wrote the news home to her father.

"It will give you a charming jaunt," her father replied testily, because he was investing money in the project. "It will teach you expert housekeeping, an object of the first importance to your happiness."

The flatboat trip took the Roosevelts nine months. Two weeks after they returned home Lydia increased their family with a little girl, Rosetta. During the trip Roosevelt had made arrangements for wood and coal to be stored along the riverbank at several points downstream for the steamboat he would be piloting the next year. Stopping in the few cities along the route, the Roosevelts informed everyone they met that they would return soon in a steamboat. Not one person said an encouraging word. The pilots and boatmen who had spent their lives on the rivers told Roosevelt to forget it. No one had ever seen a steamboat, but they were all sure that such an invention could never move upstream against the current in these western rivers.

The Roosevelts did not discourage easily. Soon after their

return east, when Lydia and the baby were able to travel, they were off to Pittsburgh with the plans to build the steamboat. Robert Fulton and Chancellor Livingston backed the project.

By February 1811, Roosevelt's boat was propped up on the banks of the Monongahela River about a mile upstream from the point in Pittsburgh where the three rivers meet. Zadok Cramer, publisher of a book called *The Navigator,* which warned river travelers about the islands, narrow channels, and dangers ahead, added a new paragraph to his 1811 edition:

> "There is now on foot a new mode of navigating our western waters, particularly the Ohio and Mississippi rivers. This is with boats propelled by the power of steam. This plan has been carried into successful operation on the Hudson River of New York and on the Delaware between Newcastle and Burlington. It has been stated that the one on the Hudson goes at the rate of four miles an hour against wind and tide on her route between New York and Albany, and frequently with five hundred passengers on board.
>
> "From these successful experiments there can be but little doubt of the plan succeeding on our western waters and proving of enough advantage to the commerce of our country. . . . It will be a novel sight . . . to see a huge boat working her way up the windings of the Ohio without the appearance of a sail, pull, or any manual labor about her—moving within the secrets of her own wonderful mechanism, and propelled by power undiscoverable."

The "huge boat" was 138 feet along the keel and christened the *New Orleans.* Building it was slow because time and again floods carried off the timber that the workmen had cut from the nearby forests. Twice the floods almost carried off the *New Orleans.* As soon as the river was free of ice in March, the boat was launched. But it was not nearly ready to leave, and by July the river was closed. Downstream travelers had to plan to move with the spring floods to avoid going aground, but this year the river had been much lower than usual.

People mumbled about strange "feelings." A comet had appeared in the sky, and no one could be sure what dreadful things comets warned of. The Roosevelts' friends all tried to talk Nicholas out of taking his wife along on such a dangerous trip. Lydia was about to have their second child.

"This is utter folly, if not absolute madness," said the kindest of Roosevelt's friends. "You have no right to peril your wife's life, no matter how reckless you may be of your own."

But, given the choice, Lydia refused to stay behind. When the *New Orleans* finally left Pittsburgh on Sunday, October 21, 1811, Lydia stood on the deck waving to the thousands of people lining the shore. The *New Orleans* headed upriver first, impressing the watchers with one last demonstration that the steamboat really could go against the current. Then, making a wide circle, it headed downstream at such a clip that everyone agreed "she must be going ten miles an hour."

The explosions of steam coming from the boiler brought people to the riverbank long after the city was left behind. The Roosevelts learned later that the Indians who saw the steamboat heading downriver that day had called it a "Fire Canoe." They were sure that the sparks flying out of its chimney were somehow related to the fiery comet they had seen earlier in the year. Word of the Fire Canoe spread from tribe to tribe downstream faster than the boat moved.

When the *New Orleans* snorted its way into the town of Wheeling (then in Virginia), Roosevelt dropped anchor and invited the town's residents to come aboard and see it for twenty-five cents each. Hundreds of people were rowed out. Many had traveled overland for days just to see this "modern marine curiosity." They were not disappointed.

Since the boat was built to be a passenger packet someday, running between New Orleans and Natchez, it looked very large in the river. People touched its boilers with respect. They tramped through its two cabins to see how the Roosevelts, their baby, a captain, an engineer, a pilot, six crewmen, two female servants, a waiter, a cook, and an immense Newfoundland dog named Tiger, could find space to live. The Roosevelts lived in the after cabin, which later would become the ladies' cabin. The gentlemen's cabin forward was much larger, and all the others lived there. The visitors were surprised to see that Lydia had made curtains, found a piece of carpet for her floor, and hung a looking glass. Their own lives were so frugal that they had given up such frills when they left the East. They asked the young couple about the trip ahead for them—How long would it take them to reach Cincinnati? What were they going to do when they reached the dreaded Falls of the Ohio beyond Louisville? And did they know the horrors ahead for them as they descended the swift-flowing Mississippi?

Starting downstream again the next day, the *New Orleans* had to round up on a lee shore twice a day. Tying the boat to a tree, the crew went out and cut wood to keep the steam boiler going. Occasionally Roosevelt found the coal that he had arranged for on the earlier trip.

A week after leaving Pittsburgh, the steamboat passed by the city of Cincinnati at a twelve-mile-per-hour clip. The townspeople waiting along the banks were impressed, but bitterly disappointed that the boat had not stopped.

"Well, he has made good his word and come to see us. But we will never see *that* boat again," said the people of Cincinnati.

The *New Orleans* arrived in Louisville, Kentucky, at midnight the end of October. The moon shone brilliantly and it was almost as light as day. The riverfront was filled with townspeople who had heard the loud chugging engine. Some woke from a sound sleep, thinking that perhaps the comet was back, and the sight of sparks flying from the boat gave their sleepy minds the idea that the comet had fallen in the river. Lydia and Nicholas were surprised to see so many people waiting for them at midnight. By now they were so used to the loud engine they had forgotten what it must sound like to others. Two days later their little boy, Henry Latrobe Roosevelt, was born.

The river was too low for them to pass over the Falls of the Ohio. Here was a drop of twenty-two feet within two miles. Every foot of that drop was booby-trapped with huge boulders that could smash a boat twice the size of the *New Orleans,* shelves of sharp black rock, whirlpools, and violent currents that could turn the boat sideways before the helmsman could turn his wheel. Roosevelt wisely decided to wait for higher water.

One night he invited his Louisville friends out to the boat for dinner. During the meal the guests chatted about how easily the *New Orleans* had traveled downstream, remarking that surely it would not be the case if the boat were going the opposite direction. When the diners had almost finished, they suddenly heard a low rumbling sound and felt the boat moving.

"The anchor line's broken!" shouted one.

"We're slipping . . . the Falls!" yelled another as the diners leaped from their chairs and raced toward the hatchway.

The boat was moving, but not downstream toward the Falls. Roosevelt, who came out on deck last, had a good laugh and told his friends he knew of no other way to convince them except to take a moonlight ride up the river. In later days many other townspeople lined up for the chance to ride upstream in the first steamboat for a dollar each.

Late in November, the *New Orleans* steamed back upstream to visit Cincinnati. The Ohioans had never expected to see the boat again. Ringing bells, popping guns, and loud cheers greeted this surprising appearance. The Roosevelts stayed a week visiting their friends and then headed once more back to Louisville. The water was still too low. There had been no rain, and soon the ice would fill the harbor. They might be stuck there until spring.

At last, on December 8, came word that the river had risen just a little. Roosevelt had five inches of water between the boat's bottom and the rocks. He decided to leave at once.

The day of leaving was strange. The sun had risen like a red globe in a gray sky. The air felt leaden, but it had felt that way for several days. Stories reached the travelers of strange doings in the forests. The forest animals had an unexplained spirit of recklessness—one day a large group of squirrels had dashed headlong into the river for no apparent reason and drowned. Even Nicholas felt the strangeness and tried to talk Lydia into taking the babies by stagecoach to a place downstream called Shippingport. This was at the lower end of the falls, where boats that could not be pulled up the falls dropped anchor and unloaded. Again Lydia refused to leave his side, although she did send the children with a maid by stagecoach to meet them later. When the *New Orleans* left the wharf at Louisville, all hands were on deck, grasping the nearest object for support. Tiger cowered as close as he could to Lydia's feet.

A falls pilot, hired just to take the boat through the rapids, headed the *New Orleans* toward the deepest channel and pointed downstream. In order to be steered, the steamboat had to be able to move faster than the current. Since the water moved fourteen miles an hour, the steam engine had to move the *New Orleans'* wheels faster than they had ever turned before. The safety valve of the boiler shrieked. The shore was crowded with silent watchers. The captains and crews of boats above the falls, who had been waiting for better conditions to make their own trips through the roaring water, were holding their breath.

The *New Orleans* sped full steam over the rocky ledges. Spray flew over the deck. The boat headed downward through eddies and whirlpools, veering suddenly to avoid crashing into rocks that thrust up from the rushing water, scraping the wooden bottom. The passage lasted through forty-five minutes of breathless plunging, and then the *New Orleans* rounded up at the bottom of the falls in deep water.

For a brief moment the boat shuddered. Had they hit bottom? The passengers all felt a sort of seasickness, then the feeling was gone. It was just nervousness, Lydia thought. Later that night, the boat shook with small shocks, but in the morning after the steam engine began shaking the passengers, no one noticed the feeling again.

"It's probably just an earthquake," Nicholas said, wondering why it lasted so long. The Roosevelts had no way of knowing that they were just entering the area where an earthquake was about to create havoc.

At 2 A.M. on the morning of December 16, a powerful quake shook the Mississippi Valley from Canada to the Gulf of Mexico. Between then and daylight more than fifty shocks were felt. At 7 A.M. came another powerful quake. This time it was recorded as far away as Venezuela. The hills shook in Asheville, North Carolina. In Charleston, South Carolina, the quaking shook the bells until they rang. Buildings swayed in New York City, and clocks stopped. A large lake disappeared completely and a new one, Reelfoot Lake, fifty miles long, formed. (It is now three miles long.) In Knoxville, Tennessee, a mountain ripped open. Sections of the Mississippi River changed course.

The Roosevelts had left before 7 A.M. and, because of the regular vibration of the boat, did not feel that particular quake. Later that day they stopped at Henderson, Kentucky, where they tied up for the night.

They were surprised to find the natives there walking around in a state of shock. Chimneys had been knocked down and trees had fallen over. Beyond Henderson were mostly Indian villages and Lydia had planned to do some shopping, but with the village of Henderson in such a state she thought it better to put off provisioning the boat until they were farther along. Through the night the boat rocked with small shocks. They did not go unnoticed because, before each one, Tiger put his head flat on the deck and moaned woefully.

Leaving Henderson the next day, the Roosevelts found things not better, but worse. As they neared the Mississippi the pilot pointed out signs that the river ahead of them was in flood. Water had overflowed into the woods, and Chickasaw Indians paddled their canoes under the trees. The steam engine had to work harder and the wheels turned more laboriously, even though the boat was still moving downstream.

Once a large canoe filled with angry-looking Indians tried to catch up to the boat. The boat was struggling through the water, barely moving as fast as a horse, when Roosevelt ordered the engineer to put on more steam quickly. The race was close for a while, but gradually the steamboat pulled ahead. The pilot warned of the danger of hitting a snag traveling at such a speed, and they slowed down when the Indians finally gave up the chase and turned their canoe back into the forest. That night Roosevelt was awakened by a pounding of feet on the deck. He raced outside, ancient sword in hand, thinking the Indians had come on board. He found the men forward fighting a fire because a servant had left green wood too close to the stove. Lydia was relieved that there were no

Indians, but some of the lovely wooden panelwork had been completely ruined.

The boat was now sixty miles above New Madrid, the town where Lydia had hoped to buy supplies for the rest of the voyage. The earthquake had been rumbling for three days. Nothing looked right. The banks were falling and trees stood upright in the middle of the river as if they had been planted there. At one place stood trees with no branches at all, leaning as if some giant wave had swept upstream. They looked for New Madrid, which had stood on a high bluff, but when they reached the spot, the land was fifteen feet lower. The town had disappeared and a huge lake lay behind where it should have been. There was no place to land even if the Roosevelts had wanted to.

Each day now the steamboat passengers met people along the river who begged to be taken aboard. They told of their homes falling down, great holes opening in the ground, and cottonwood trees being swallowed up by the water. One man in a flatboat said he had wakened one morning to a loud roaring and hissing sound.

"The waters suddenly boiled up in huge swells," he said, his voice still quivering as he tried to explain what he didn't understand. "The boat rocked so badly we could hardly keep on our feet. On shore the earth opened into wide holes and then closed so suddenly that water and sand and mud flew up in jets higher than the trees."

Aboard the *New Orleans* was a strange silence. The crewmen spoke in whispers. Tiger prowled around growling. No one slept well. Then one night when the boat was fastened to the shore of "Island No. 32" strange noises sounded all around the boat. More hard objects than usual seemed to hit the boat below the waterline. Scratching sounds and gurgling water added to the nightmares of the weary, half-asleep crew. In the morning the first person up on deck gave a loud shout. Everyone turned out fast. At first their reason told them the anchor had slipped and the boat had moved down the river. But the pilot pointed out familiar sights on shore. Geese and ducks were flying aimlessly, squawking in the air. The water, thick and red with mud, was covered with foam. "Island No. 32" had completely disappeared.

The pilot, Andrew Jack, was now thoroughly confused. He had lived all his life as a boatman on these waters, but the changes from the earthquakes were so great that he no longer had any idea where they were. Where he expected deep water, there were roots and stumps. Tall trees had disappeared and the islands that were still in place had changed their shapes completely. Where the main passage appeared to be, the water became a dead-end pool. Other boatmen on the river were just as confused.

There was nothing for the *New Orleans* to do but to go on. Eventually the crew managed to find the way downstream out of the area where the earthquake had done its worst. The *New Orleans* arrived in Natchez just after Christmas. On that same day Lydia's maid and Nicholas Baker, the engineer, were the first couple ever to be married on board a steamboat. The Fire Canoe's troubles had come to an end.

On January 10, 1812, the *New Orleans* arrived in its namesake city, amid cheers of crowds and a welcome by the governor. One very important bale of cotton was aboard as cargo—the first of millions of bales to follow. Soon the steamboat began regular trips with passengers who gladly paid $18 to go downstream to New Orleans in two or three days, and $25 to travel upstream to Natchez in seven or eight. The fares paid for over half the cost of the steamboat in its first year.

As for the dangerous Falls of the Ohio, the steamboat *Buffalo* proved, in April 1817, that steamboats could go up the falls as well as down. A canal was soon built around the falls, however, making it safer for all kinds of boats.

Chesapeake Bay and Pleasure Parties

In 1815 the new capital city of Washington was enjoying a poor reputation. So were steamboats. Steamboats disappointed people because they sometimes exploded or caught fire. Washington City disappointed people because it looked like a lot of empty streets with a few big buildings. Someone had the idea of putting the two together.

On May 24, 1815, the steamboat *Washington,* Captain O'Neale, arrived in Washington City by way of the Potomac River. Incredibly it had left New York City just a week before and had steamed only fifty-two hours. A few years before, the same trip by horse would have taken ten days. Now those people who had said the United States capital was out of touch with the rest of the country would have to eat their words. The few bad roads leading to the capital city would soon be improved, and where they could not be, why not use steamboats?

The *Washington,* according to the newspaper, was meant to carry travelers from the capital "to Potowmac Creek, where the passengers will land and proceed to Fredericksburg, Virginia, by which means all the bad road between those two cities will be avoided." The idea was sound, but people still took a very dim view of noisy, chuffing steamboats as a means of travel.

The steamboat company owners took a long look at Chesapeake Bay. The bay was not given to wild storms and pounding waves like the ocean. People might take trips on the bay who would never have set foot on an ocean-going vessel. And so began the "parties of pleasure"—to build up confidence in steamboats.

A new Steamboat Hotel and Boarding House opened in Norfolk the following May. It offered sea breezes and a "healthful climate" to the people who lived in mid-Atlantic cities. Every day at the ordinary table, customers could have mock turtle soup for 37 cents, gravy 25 cents, beefsteak 37 cents, venison 30 cents, opened oysters 25 cents, "fryed" oysters 37 cents, stewed oysters 37 cents, and spirits for 12 cents a half-pint glass.

The steamboats that carried vacationers to the new hotel tried to outdo each other in offering comforts to their passengers. With a "getting there is half the fun" attitude, they put bars into their boats, added copper low-pressure boilers (they do not blow up as easily as high-pressure boilers), and advertised dancing parties on a deck covered over with an awning. Soon a boat added a library, claiming that the vibration from the engine was so slight that the customer could easily hold a book and read. One boat heading for Old Point Comfort, Virginia, must have provided its three hundred passengers with a less than restful trip. On the lower deck there was dancing to a band playing cotillion music. In the main saloon a musical and dramatic soirée took place, while a military band played continuously on the upper deck.

Boats became larger and more luxurious. The largest in the United States in 1817 was the steamboat *Virginia,* Captain John Ferguson. This boat had been built to shorten the distance between Baltimore and Norfolk. It covered the distance in twenty-four hours, while a packet schooner took three days. Travelers who hated shifting baggage from one stagecoach to another and who remembered having to leave the table when the stagecoach driver was ready to go, whether they had eaten dinner or not, began to look again at water travel. Not only could they have a healthy voyage, but they could even take their own carriages and horses along to use when they disembarked. And if that still was not enough to convince a reluctant water traveler, the steamboat company advertised that Captain Ferguson was "a skillful, urbane, and gentlemanly" person who employed only men of character on his ship.

From the decks of the steamboat *Virginia,* one passenger watched an exhibition by Mr. Meyer, inventor of the famous Life Preserving Dress. For just seventy-five cents the trip ten miles out from Norfolk provided a sort of seagoing circus party.

"Two men showed off the Life Preserving Dress by walking in the water as upright as if on shore," said the passenger. "They proved their ability to eat and drink. Then they loaded and discharged pistols and fenced with swords while wearing the amazing outfit."

Now that pleasure parties had caught on, the steamboat companies looked for new party ideas. In 1820, so many people wanted to visit the *Columbia,* a "tall ship," lying at Hampton Roads, that it seemed natural to send them out on a ship. The steamer *Richmond* carried hundreds of people out to see "the 74" (it was a 74-gun ship of the line) for one dollar each. Other steamers began carrying families and their servants (half price) to camp meetings at Hampton and to vacation spots on the water's edge.

A fleet of forty-five schooners, sloops, and steamboats was needed to carry all the pleasure parties up the James River in late May 1822. James-Town was having a jubilee to celebrate its two hundredth anniversary as America's first settlement. All afternoon the boats arrived with visitors, each boat greeted by a gunshot from the artillery. Everyone visited the site of the ancient church of old James-Town, but there were no signs of where the old village stood which a tourist can see today. At that time an arbor ran all the way from the landing at the river up to the ancient manor house. The ladies had seats under the covered arbor to hear the orators for the day. A band of music

played patriotic songs, Mrs. Green gave a vocal concert, and the young folks danced. Mr. Warrell was there with his "Picturesque Theater," to which he had added new scenes showing Captain John Smith, Powhatan's village, and even Pocahontas. As the two thousand pleasure party-goers left for home that night, hundreds of rockets lit up the sky, creating a sight to behold.

Two days later the Hygeia Hotel, named for the goddess of health, opened on the fortifications at Old Point Comfort. Sitting at the very crossroads of the steamboat lanes, the hotel bragged that it saved its clients a great deal of money because they could not use horses and carriages there. For the invalid —a condition that was very fashionable then—the hotel offered sea breezes and relief from "moschetos." For the man of leisure, there was fine fishing at the Rip Raps. The studious person or recluse could walk on the pebbled beach. For the young lady, the hotel had only to mention that the delights of a military fort, complete with military bands, uniforms, and weekly cotillions, were nearby. The vacationer or family could swim and enjoy the hard sandy beaches where there were bathhouses for the ladies. A small house on the grounds had four "apartments" where the delicate could take daily warm saltwater baths. The icehouse was filled with clean "northern" ice, and the hotel imported a constant supply of Juniper Water from the Dismal Swamp. Best of all, the hotel offered daily pleasure party trips by steamboat to Cape Charles and Cape Henry, where the Chesapeake Bay meets the ocean.

Chained Spirit with Fire Under

While travelers warmed up to steamboats on the inland sea that is Chesapeake Bay, the government experimented with a few steamboats of its own in the West. An expedition under

Major Stephen Harriman Long was sent out in 1819, mainly to establish military posts to protect the fur trade and to control the Indians. The Indians may have had a second sense about the steamboat with a serpent's head on the bow. When they first saw it they gave it a name.

"White man bad man," they said. "Keep a great spirit chained and build fire under it to make it work a boat."

Titian Ramsay Peale was a teenager when he was hired to go along as one of the expedition's artists.

"You'd better start practising," teased his brother Rembrandt Peale. "You're good at drawing dead animals that don't move. Wait until you try live ones. Get some practice drawing landscapes, too. And don't forget to make notes on the spot. Notes written at the time have always an interest and accuracy that distant recollections never have."

Fortunately Peale took his brother's advice, because the notes he made tell an interesting story of the Long expedition to Fort Osage (just outside of today's Independence, Missouri). The steamboat, christened the *Western Engineer,* was built in Pittsburgh, Pennsylvania, and sailed from there on May 3, 1819.

The *Western Engineer* was not the best steamboat ever built. It cost the government a great deal of money in the end. Its paddle wheels were in the stern to lessen the chance of snagging on an underwater tree, and it floated in only two and a half feet of water. The steersman sat in a bulletproof house on the quarterdeck. One wheel was named for James Monroe, and the other for J. C. Calhoun, the two engineers responsible for the expedition. A mast with a square sail and a topsail came in handy when the wind blew from the right direction. On the bow was a brass four-pounder cannon. The wheels and sides were armed with four brass howitzers which had been used by General Wayne in the Indian wars. Thirty men sailed on the

Titian Peale sketched the *Western Engineer* in 1819
at the start of its daring river adventures

boat—ten soldiers, ten crewmen, and ten others including the artists, mechanic, and a doctor.

The boat had been carefully planned to fit everything into the smallest space. A bench around the main cabin not only provided seating, but all the clothing was stored inside it. Lockers above the bench stored books. Even the dining table could be taken apart to form small writing desks, according to Titian Peale.

The most unusual feature about the boat was the huge serpent that formed its bow. The serpent's neck was black and scaly; its head was as high as the deck. The body sloped beneath the water to give the appearance of carrying the boat on its back. The exhaust to eject the steam from the engine was placed in the serpent's mouth, so that it puffed steam constantly when the boiler was heated. The serpent impressed young Peale as well as the Indians.

The *Western Engineer*'s crew gave a twenty-two-gun salute to the cheering crowd that gathered in Pittsburgh to watch the departure.

"A commissioner of the Bible Society visited the boat and left us with two Bibles and one or two other books for the good of our souls," said Peale.

When the steamboat reached Cincinnati, the crew had plenty of time to read the books while waiting nine days for repairs to the steam engine. The mechanic suggested some changes, but there was no time to wait for parts to be sent from the East. The government was anxious for its steamboat to get on with the trip. By May 30, the *Western Engineer* reached the Mississippi River and began its ten-day slow journey up that river to St. Louis.

When the boat moved too slowly for its impatient passengers, they hopped off and hiked across land to meet the boat at the next bend in the river. On these hiking trips Peale discovered that he was a good shot and often brought back fresh deer or turkey meat. Going aground also gave the men exercise. All hands jumped into the water then and tried to warp the boat off with ropes and anchor.

Now that they were heading northward, the wind sometimes helped fill the sail. One day the boat was sailing along very fast when it struck a snag. The water began coming in on the cabin floor and all hands were set to pumping. After pumping all night, they found the leak and ran the *Western Engineer* onto a sandbar to repair the hole. Titian had a day off and went fishing.

Before many miles, the Mississippi began showing what it could do with a steamboat that tried chugging upstream against the muddy current. At a rapid section of the river the *Western Engineer* could not raise enough steam to move forward at all. The mechanic found the boilers filled with mud.

"We can't use this muddy water in the boilers," groaned the engineer, knowing very well it was the only water they could get.

From this point in the trip, the boat had to stop every few days to clean the mud out of the boilers. The mud also took its toll on the valves, polishing them so smoothly that they had to be reground several times.

Above St. Louis, the expedition turned into the Missouri River. The "Big Muddy" made the Mississippi look clean.

"Too thick to drink and too thin to plow," said a local farmer, and the men agreed.

The river current was often so fast that the steamboat could move only one mile in an hour. On July 7 the boat ran onto a sandbar and was surrounded by snags, sawyers, and floating logs. Just as they were trying to get off, the main steam cock blew out with a tremendous explosion.

"It alarmed us considerable," said Peale, "thinking it was the boiler that had bursted."

The next day they made very little speed, because it was 90° in the coolest part of the boat. The men working near the steam engine had to escape to the deck to keep from passing out.

"We finally stopped at 4 P.M., it being too warm for the men to stand on the deck without an awning to shelter them from the sun."

Another day the boat moved only two miles, although the day was not an entire loss.

"One man found a bee tree with more than seven gallons of honey, two large buckets full," said Peale, whose teenage appetite had not been satisfied since he had left home.

At long last the *Western Engineer* made its sluggish way to Fort Osage by sundown on August 1. A party of men who had left the boat miles back had already reached the fort several days earlier by walking.

Although the expedition found the Missouri River far too muddy to use for passenger steamboats, the *Western Engineer,* with its fiery serpent bow, amazed and thrilled several thousand settlers who saw it go by, flying the American flag in territory that was far from their eastern roots. They were cheered as they broke soil and built new homes in the land they had found. The steamboat's coming had made them feel a part of a large united country.

It was just as well, however, that they did not read Major Long's description of the soil they were so proud of.

"The Great American Desert," he said, referring to the land between the Mississippi River and the Rocky Mountains, "is almost wholly unfit for cultivation, and of course uninhabitable by a people depending upon agriculture . . . but it makes a frontier barrier against enemies."

A Novel Voyage Around Long Island

"It is not considered healthy to remain many weeks at a time in town while the hot weather lasts," said Jacob Harvey's doctor when Jacob moved to New York in 1820.

Harvey believed in following a doctor's advice, so on the ninth of August he signed up with a group of travelers for a three-day "novel voyage" on the steamboat *Robert Fulton,* Captain Cahoone. A novel voyage was the New York term for a pleasure trip.

"This is the finest steamboat in our waters," Jacob said to himself as he climbed the gangplank.

The steamboat was rigged with sails to use when the wind

was fair, but its steam engine was belching long streamers of steam in the breeze. At precisely 9 A.M. Captain Cahoone gave the signal to leave. He stood on the wheel housing giving signals with his trumpet. Spectators along the wharf broke into applause. The ship's band played "Hail Columbia" and "Yankee Doodle" over and over. Jacob wondered if the band knew any other tunes.

One hundred and forty passengers crowded the railing, enjoying the fine breeze. The ladies clustered beneath the boat's awning so they would not spoil their pale complexions. Within an hour the boat had passed through the Narrows and met its first ocean waves. Many ladies turned noticeably paler, including one lady whom Jacob had been eyeing all morning.

"The railings of the ship were now pressed by many a delicate arm," Jacob wrote in his journal later, trying hard to be poetic. The fact was he had never seen so many beautiful girls all vomiting. He was especially sympathetic toward Julia—he heard her name for the first time now. She had come aboard all vivacious and jolly.

"Now," Jacob thought sadly as he watched her at the railing, "she looks pale, bilious, and . . . well, interesting."

Surrounded by several comforters who just made her feel worse, Julia hurried with several others down to their berths below. Jacob was left on the deck filled with young men, some greener than others. They watched the ship *Benjamin* go by with all sails set, and the band played one of its two specialties in the sailing ship's honor. In the distance they watched the streamers of black smoke as the steamer *Franklin* headed out to sea. A revenue cutter approached and politely sent over some bait. Some of the men got out their fishing poles.

"Will we anchor off the banks of Long Island to fish?" they asked the captain hopefully.

"Too rough to anchor," Cahoone answered curtly.

At 2 P.M. the steamboat arrived off Long Branch on the New Jersey coast. The captain hoisted his flag as a signal for skiffs to put out from shore to take the passengers in to spend a few hours on the beach. Some of the ladies crept weakly up to the deck in the hope of being first on shore. But the signal from shore indicated that it was too rough for the skiffs to venture out. The passengers on this day had to be content with looking at the vacation resort with spyglasses.

Long Branch, a favorite with Philadelphia vacationers, was now becoming the "in" place for New Yorkers who could

The ladies' flag is up, and it's time for their swim at Long Branch, N.J., a favorite resort for New Yorkers to reach by steamboat

reach it easily by a healthful sea voyage. From its two large hotels, bathers could watch every ship that left New York harbor. The ladies were allowed to swim until 11 A.M., when the red flag was hoisted for the men to swim. Even though families came together to the resort, it would have been shocking for men and women to swim together.

The band swung into its two specialties again as the ship turned out to sea and headed for the Long Island shore. The ladies disappeared without a sound.

"The waves were tossing us from side to side," Jacob wrote in his journal. The few men who were left went below at 3 P.M. for a dinner of roast beef, leg of mutton, boiled chicken, Irish potatoes, and Virginia ham. Although it was not really the dinner hour, the captain had learned from long experience that serving the big meal when the boat headed into waves would save him a great deal of food and money.

Jacob spent the afternoon without much enjoyment. The ladies were all sick and the men filled the cabin with cigar smoke. The ship rolled exceedingly and heavy showers of spray came over the deck.

When it came time to draw lots for berths, it was obvious that there were not nearly enough. Jacob managed to draw one, but discovered he was to share it with a little boy. The boy's father sidled up to Jacob.

"That's my son," he said proudly. "My but he has a terrible fashion of kicking in his sleep. I wish you luck."

Then he kindly suggested trading tickets with Jacob—and that is how Jacob ended up sleeping on a chair with one blanket, the man slept in the berth, and the boy slept on the floor. Men were sleeping all over the cabin. They were on the tables, under the tables, in the chairs, and on the floor.

"What an idea we have of pleasure!" groaned Jacob.

He was on deck by 5 A.M. to watch the sun rise. The ship was still rolling, but in the distance he could see the village of Southampton. Within a few hours they passed Montauk lighthouse, and the waters in Block Island Sound were calm enough so that a few of the young ladies appeared. Jacob regained interest in the voyage.

"We were called to breakfast—rather, to a trial of skill," he moaned, "to see who could obtain tea and bread from the tardy and insolent waiters."

The tables were set out on the deck, and, amid the hubbub of everyone shouting for mugs, forks instead of spoons, cups of tea instead of coffee or chocolate, there was not much peace. After breakfast the ship dropped anchor off Gardiner's Island so the men could fish for half an hour.

The entertainment that had been advertised before the ship sailed turned out to be a little boy named Smyth. Smyth, about ten years old, was dressed in Grecian robes, a band of flowers on his brow. For what seemed like an hour he recited the words of Alexander the Great at a feast given in his honor. Jacob was far more interested in getting acquainted with Julia.

The ship pulled into the harbor of New London, Connecticut, later in the afternoon. Once again the band struck up its two well-rehearsed tunes. As the boat passed Fort Trumbull, the soldiers stationed there fired a one-gun salute and gave three cheers. When the boat neared the town wharf, all the townspeople leaned from windows or stood on the dock shouting loud "Huzzas." While the gentlemen escorted the ladies on a two-hour tour of the village, the townspeople toured the steamboat. Julia regained some of her vivacity, even telling Jacob that the ladies were planning to have a dance that evening, providing the band could play something danceable.

The boat sailed out of the harbor about suppertime, and a large crowd was ready for food this time. The service was worse than before. There were not nearly enough seats or even enough plates. To make matters worse, the band members had stubbornly sat themselves down to be served first.

"Leave the table," ordered Captain Cahoone. "The tourists are served first on my ship."

The bandleader was furious, and the players refused to play another note during the rest of the voyage. Jacob was not sorry to hear this, but the ladies set up such a wail about the cotillion they had planned that, after a great deal of arguing and bargaining, the bandleader finally agreed to play "for the ladies."

The dance was a success, but it was rudely interrupted by another duel of words—this time with the captain.

"What time do we reach New Haven?" asked one of the men.

The captain's answer was somewhat muffled, but it sounded something like "We won't be going to New Haven."

"The advertisement says this boat goes to New Haven."

"With this tide we cannot get within a mile and a half of the wharf," said the captain angrily. "We are not going there."

"This line *always* goes to New Haven," argued the tourists.

"If we stop there, we cannot go through Hurl Gate until Sunday morning," the captain retorted. Hurl Gate (known in less polite company as Hell Gate) was a wild, narrow passage between huge rocks, which could not be passed except during certain tides. It had been only a few years since the first steamboat had managed to go through the Hurl Gate waters at all.

The tourists were all in a confusion. Jacob said later, "In a few moments, we were all speakers and none hearers."

"This is a Republican country," shouted one tourist who had been louder than the others. "Therefore we will vote and the majority wins."

Loud agreements followed this suggestion, and, when the question was put to a vote, the majority voted to stop at New Haven. Captain Cahoone retired to his walkway over the paddle wheels where passengers were not allowed to go. The dancers finally gave out about midnight and fell asleep, dreaming of their day's outing in New Haven. When they awoke at five in the morning, they discovered that New Haven was forty miles behind them. The pilot claimed he got lost in a fog, then he said the captain had changed his orders. An angry group of men called on Captain Cahoone, charging him with unconstitutional conduct.

"I am a Republican on shore," he said firmly. "But on board ship I am the boss."

The disgruntled tourists had to be content with watching the shoreline come gradually closer as they approached the end of Long Island Sound. At least the ladies had all fully recuperated. But when the anticipated afternoon's entertainment turned out to be young Master Smyth again, dressed as King Richard III and trailing a sword taller than himself as he quoted lines from Shakespeare, the pleasure party had some very unpleasant words to say. Going through Hurl Gate, getting bumped by a sloop in the whirlpool, was the most exciting happening of the day. By eleven thirty Saturday night the boat docked in New York. Jacob and Julia had found a mutual friend who would give them a proper introduction.

The Bad News About Steamboats

By 1820 the competition was no longer between steamboats and horses, but between steamboats of rival companies. Sometimes the anger between rivals was so intense that the companies did not care at all about the comfort of their passengers. That summer, New York State refused to let New Jersey State steamboats in their waters, and of course New Jersey kept out New York boats. Unfortunately, the poor traveler who wished to travel between the two states was hustled into a large rowboat and rowed over the bay to Staten Island. There he had to board another large rowboat, manned by rowers from the other state, and be taken over the water to board the steamboat to continue his trip. Sometimes the captain of a New York boat took his passengers just to the closest point of New Jersey land and dumped them there, saying there would be stagecoaches to take them on to their destinations. He then steamed away quickly before they discovered that no stagecoaches were waiting.

Often the rivalry took a more dangerous form. No two Americans on horseback or holding the reins of rival stagecoach teams had been able to resist a race. Neither could steamboat captains.

Two such rivals carried passengers from Norfolk up the James River to Richmond in 1823. Each line kept lowering its prices. The trip cost $5 on the steamboat *Potomac* of the Potomac Line. When the James River Steamboat Line could not afford to compete, it advertised that passengers could travel free on the days that the Potomac Line sailed up to Richmond. Delighted passengers lined up for the free trip. But on August 10 the rivalry was no longer funny.

The *Richmond* of the James River Line was lying to in shoal waters off Wind Mill Point, landing some passengers. Coming up behind, too close for comfort, was the steamer *Potomac.* Captain Coffin of the *Richmond* ordered his boat to move straight ahead, because it looked as if the *Potomac* meant to ram his boat. The *Potomac* came straight on, hitting the *Richmond* hard on its port side, splintering the rail and crushing one of the lifeboats.

Steamboat captains were no more friendly on the Hudson River. There Sally Donaldson, her brother and his wife, and her friends Abby and Kitty Cooper, were taking a pleasant summer trip to Albany.

"The contests between two steam boat concerns was at its height," Sally explained. "The fare from New York to Albany, an overnight trip that included dinner and tea, was only two dollars."

Sally's boat and another one had been racing each other all the way up the river. Occasionally one gained when the other boat had to stop to pick up passengers from wharfs along the river. Just before reaching West Point, the ropes on the small boats broke in landing passengers from Sally's boat. Ordinarily the small boats were propelled back and forth from shore by ropes attached to the steam engine. When those ropes broke, the sailors had to use the oars to row passengers to and from shore. This slowed down their boat, which had been ahead up to now. Soon the other steamboat gained on them.

Sally's boat stopped to unload passengers at West Point, when suddenly the other boat churned up between Sally's boat and the shore, endangering all the passengers.

"Our bow struck the rival boat and the shock was sensibly felt by us both," Sally said. "Some ladies fainted. Others wept. But unconscious of any real cause for alarm, Kitty, Abby, and I sat with the composure of heroines. One poor young lady in the alarm threw herself into the boat for West Point. She did not recover her self possession until the captain was handing her up to the dock. Then she demanded to know where she was and, since she said she had not planned to get off at West Point, had to be escorted back to the ship."

Isaac Fidler was on another steamboat heading for Albany when he noticed a boat of greater power coming up behind.

"This is a far better boat," claimed the captain, who was standing next to Fidler. "I could beat it anytime I choose."

As soon as the other boat came near, the captain suddenly ordered more steam and a change in direction to cross the other boat's course. Having tried that and succeeded, he ordered his helmsman to cross the rival boat's course again. This time, however, the captain of the larger boat ordered his own helmsman to hit the smaller boat in the side.

"A tremendous crash followed," said Fidler, still rubbing his elbow. "It carried away the rail work of half the side as well as one of the small boats. Bars of iron an inch thick were bent and twisted like slender wires. The captains, crews, and passengers on the two boats all shook threatening fists, and those on the victorious boat bragged about their captain's prowess."

Finally, in 1840, the courts forbade such behavior and prohibited the racing of boats. Any race that ended in loss of life could send the boat's captain to prison for ten years or cost him a $5,000 fine.

The worst that could happen to a steamboat was an explosion of its steam boiler. Since the steam boilers were under high pressure, explosions were fairly common. Most of them happened when the captain allowed the steam to be kept up while the boat was not moving forward. Then, at the first move of the paddle wheel, the boiler could blow the boat to bits.

Such an accident happened to the steamer *Moselle* on April 25, 1838. The *Moselle* was a "brag boat"—one that was new, elegant, and fast. Captain Perkins had just spent the day in Cincinnati telling everyone what a fine boat he had. Many who listened to him had signed on for the trip to St. Louis. Captain Perkins got up steam as the boat left the wharf. He was a little annoyed because a rival boat had taken off just before him. Another annoyance was having to stop to pick up a family that was waiting in the river on a raft. But Perkins figured it would

When a steamboat exploded, the men were the ones most likely to be burned, and the ladies often drowned in their huge skirts

Entered according to Act of Congress in the year 1859, by FRANK LESLIE, in the Clerk's Office of the District Court for the Southern District of New York.

. 181.—VOL. VII.] NEW YORK, SATURDAY, MAY 21, 1859. [PRICE 6 CENTS

EXPLOSION OF THE ST. NICHOLAS.

day the 24th April, the steamboat St. Nicholas, a regular boat between St. Louis and New Orleans, exploded her , causing death and injuries of a most frightful character to a umber of her passengers.

EXCITEMENT OF THE LADIES ON THE ALARM OF FIRE.

MISS KENNEDY CLINGING BY A RINGBOLT TO THE WRECK.

The accident happened at Island 60, about seven miles below the scene of the destruction of the Pennsylvania.

The vessel and cargo were a total loss; the boat having taken fire and burnt to the water's edge immediately after the explosion.

The number of lives lost would have been largely increased but for the fortunate circumstance that the steamer Susquehanna but a few miles below at the time of the explosion, and she soon alongside the wreck, and rendered all the assistance that possible in saving those who escaped injury and in rescuing

A LADY JUMPING WITH HER TWO CHILDREN FROM THE BURNI VESSEL.

Wooden steamboats burned quickly, because the big saloon in the center acted like a chimney to draw the flames not take long to get the family aboard, and he kept up steam while they climbed onto the lower deck. Just as the paddle wheels began to turn, the stored-up steam exploded with a blast heard miles away.

"Heads, limbs, bodies and blood were seen flying through the air in every direction," reported the newspaper the next day. The boat was "torn to flinders as far back as the gentlemen's cabin." The captain was thrown into the city street, as the boat was still not more than thirty feet from shore. Another man was blown through the roof of a house. Passengers who were unhurt panicked when they discovered the boat was sinking fast. They jumped in the water and floated downriver with the current. One infant was picked up alive downstream. Within fifteen minutes the boat had disappeared and over two hundred people had died.

A new Steamboat Law was passed that year. The master of a boat was ordered to open the safety valves to keep down the steam in the boiler whenever the headway motion of the boat was stopped. Every boat was ordered to have a fire "engine" and a suction hose. And every member of every crew was charged with being responsible for the lives of the passengers. Any crew member who did not do everything possible to save a passenger's life was liable to ten years at hard labor.

Luxury on the Hudson

Steam boiler explosions had passengers so worried that steamboat companies had to give them more confidence. How better than to make the boat look luxurious? The idea worked. Surely, passengers said to themselves, if there were a chance that a boat might blow up, the company would not have spent so much money to make this boat look like a millionaire's parlor.

"The *Albany* is the most splended conveyance I ever moved in in my life," said John Fowler on August 11, 1830.

Three hundred and fifty other passengers shared his excitement on that trip up the Hudson River from New York. The trip that had once taken Fulton thirty-six hours now took only twenty. Most passengers had bought a guidebook which pointed out the "lions" along the way. The Hudson had so many "lions" worth seeing that few passengers bothered to go below until several hours had passed.

Starting in the daylight, everyone watched for such "lions" as the dueling place where Aaron Burr killed Alexander Hamilton, the high cliffs of the "Palisadoes" on the New Jersey side, and Sing Sing prison. The prison was just being built and its four stories would soon hold eight hundred prisoners in solitary cells.

"I went to visit a prison last fall," John Fowler told the man standing next to him at the rail. "The prisoners had gone to breakfast when I arrived at 6 A.M. One of the keepers showed me the cells. They were each about 3½ feet wide and seven feet long. All the furniture was a hammock which is let down in the daytime, a stool, and a Bible on a corner shelf. Then the keeper took me to see them in the dining hall. They moved in single file with a slow lockstep, standing erectly and keeping exact time. They all had to turn their faces toward the keepers to show they were not talking. No conversation is ever permitted between prisoners. They sat down at a signal given by the keepers and began eating. I would have thought it impossible for 635 men and women to eat without a sound."

On his next trip north, John Fowler took a different steamboat.

"The steamer *North America* is even more beautiful than the *Albany* was," he said as he climbed aboard the tremendous new boat. "It is as elegant and large as a palace."

The *North America* was so gigantic that its upper portion projected far out over the hull. Its decks held a library as well as a barbershop. One young man, feeling very important on his first trip, woke the barber out of a sound sleep and demanded a shave at two in the morning. The barber scraped his chin for him.

"How much?" asked the young man when he had finished.

"How much?" the barber stared down at him. "Why, sir, in general we charge, but your beard is so small that . . ."

The young man left the shop in a huff. "What an insult was this to my manhood!" he wrote in his diary later.

Like most of the luxurious steamers, the *North America* had dozens of gilded mirrors, carpets in its cabins, upholstered and cushioned seats with footstools and soft pillows. But the sides of both the ladies' and the gentlemen's cabins were lined with three rows of the same narrow sleeping berths. In the wash-

By 2 A.M. most of the steamboat passengers are tucked into their tiny berths, their boots lined up to be polished

room were the same two dirty towels to dry the hands and faces of three hundred passengers.

At three in the morning the steamboat arrived as close as possible to Albany, and the passengers transferred onto a smaller steamboat called *The Firefly*. It took them to the city wharf over water too shallow for the large steamboat. Travelers had been so used to being shuffled around in the wee hours of the morning that no one seemed to think it strange that the steamboat had not left New York City at a later hour so they could arrive at a more convenient time. The shops in Albany were almost all open and doing business by six anyway. The steamboat passengers just had time to find a hotel, wash their faces, eat breakfast, and change their clothes.

On a hot night the Hudson River boats were somewhat less than luxurious. Tyrone Power, a traveling actor from England, took a steamboat one summer night as far as Hyde Park.

"The boat was crowded, and what a scene did the cabins present," he said. "Two hundred men were stowed away in tiers of berths, lying in rows on stretchers placed close together between the decks of the steamboat on one of the hottest nights of summer." Tyrone slept on the top deck.

Meanwhile, in the ladies' cabin Fanny Kemble, stage star, was trying to get to sleep. Children always traveled in the same cabin with their mothers, and crying babies made sleep impossible. But it was the older "children" that bothered Fanny.

"At one stop three young ladies boarded. They did not plan to sleep so they giggled the whole way and chattered. No one could sleep until about 2 A.M. when the boat stopped and they got off."

To hear the other side of the story, listen to Sally Donaldson, who was traveling with two giggly friends.

"At night a most ludicrous scene commenced. The cabins were crowded, every berth occupied, and the whole floor covered with mattresses and blankets on which women and children were endeavoring to sleep. Abby and I were content to share a berth with each other, sitting in upright position opposite one another and so arranging our dresses that we could look out of a small window in our berth and see what was going on on the deck. . . . We had taken on more people at each landing and could not have room for half. For the first hour in our apartment there had been wrangling and almost quarreling for quarters, united with the crying of infants and the coughing of children. These gradually subsided. As new passengers were received, Abby and I talked to them. At 3 A.M. we put on our traveling dresses and went out on deck. Novelty made up for our lack of rest," said the teenager.

The one discomfort that Hudson River steamboat passengers did not have was mosquitoes. Those summer critters were waiting for them at the hotels along the shore. No windows had screens. And sleeping without opening the window in summer was unthinkable. Here's how one summer traveler solved the mosquito problem.

"The mosquitoes were in force. They were delighted to have a fresh subject and showed their delight in the most insinuating and piercing manner. After fighting them for one and a half hours, I played possum and allowed the whole band to cease their exciting buzzzzz and settle quietly on my face and neck. When they supposed that all opposition on my part had ceased, I killed them all with a damp towel which I had armed myself with. Not one escaped to tell the tale and bring in a fresh band, and so with a great satisfaction, I fell asleep about one o'clock."

Steaming to the Deep South

Tyrone Power hurried out into Philadelphia's dark streets one cold morning in 1834, muffled in his greatcoat, fur collar, and shawl.

"No timekeeper is so punctual as an American steamer," he groaned.

The northern steamboats left exactly when they said they would. The streets of the city were silent and deserted, except for the columns of people pressing toward the Delaware River steamboat landing. In the distance he saw pillars of dense black smoke mingled with vicious-looking lines of thin whitish vapors. Their savage hissing sound almost drowned out the bell that was calling the passengers with its last warning. The boat was surrounded by a crowd of people, some carrying carpetbags and valises up the gangplank.

Suddenly the bell and the hissing stopped. In the momentary silence the porters leaped back on shore. With a quick motion of the paddle wheel, the crewman let go of the spring line and the boat moved out into the river.

"In the next moment, we were rushing like unslipped greyhounds through the waters," Powers thought poetically. He left his watching place on the promenade deck where he had stood well aft of the boilers. If they should explode on starting up, he knew he would be safest there. He had not brought along a life preserver, but many of the ladies on board had.

As he passed the ladies' cabin, he glanced in and saw that it was decorated with gold-rimmed mirrors, carpets, and curtains—all meant to lull the fainthearted into a feeling of security. The men's cabin forward was not nearly so comfortable. He stepped into the captain's office and paid for his trip, also buying a ticket for breakfast.

Down the steps in the saloon were two long rows of tables, with every seat taken. The tables were crammed with dishes of beefsteak, ham, fish, chicken, wild game, omelets, hot rolls, cake, bread, and cups of tea and coffee. Although Power enjoyed the food when he finally found a seat, the air was poisoned by two stoves burning "iron coal" (anthracite coal) and letting off gases. He hurried back to the upper deck and its pure air.

At New Castle, Delaware, Power and the others left the steamboat and settled into seats of the Frenchtown Railroad cars. This amazingly speedy little train carried them sixteen miles in less than one hour. Soon they were boarding the steamboat *Washington* for the ride down Chesapeake Bay.

Near the mouth of the Patapsco River, Power noticed a large steamer coming toward his boat with a signal flag flying. It was the *Columbus,* bound for Norfolk. Several passengers from the *Washington* planned to go on her, rather than sail up the river to Baltimore as Power planned to do. But there was half a gale blowing and the sea was choppy. Power hurried to the bow to see how this exchange worked.

"The *Columbus* laid head to wind with just enough way on to steer her," he told his friends later. "Our ship gradually lessened speed until, as she approached the *Columbus,* she was barely moving, but coming alongside. The gangways were let down. The crew passed warps and tied the boats securely, head and stern, so that the huge vessels became as one."

Within a few minutes, the passengers and luggage had been transferred safely. Adding to the noise of the steam escaping from the safety valves of the two boats was that of a third steamboat which chose that particular moment to pass very close to them. Power expected a stampede from the horses tied on the bow of the *Columbus* in a half circle. Behind them was a double row of flashy-looking covered wagons that belonged to Yankee peddlers just starting out for their annual winter visits to the South. The peddlers managed to calm their horses until the paddles of the two boats began moving again. The lines were cast off, and the boats went on their way. The *Columbus* headed south. The *Washington* went west toward Baltimore.

"Although we had not over fourteen miles to go," said Power, "the captain was bent on overtaking the steamer that passed us . . . and he succeeded."

That night Power slept in a large hotel. He had to agree with a friend of his that although Americans liked to think of themselves as free men, they certainly were not free in their hotels.

"Their hours of getting up and eating are dictated by the hotelkeeper. He rings a bell and they come running. He places before them what he thinks proper and they swallow it without grumbling."

Power had a private room, with sheets as white as snow—most unusual in a country where most sheets were brown and used by several hotel guests before they were changed. His only complaint was the mosquitoes.

"If only they would have made peace with me," he groaned. "But oh, how they did hum and bomb and bite and buzz, and how I did fume and flap and snatch and swear!"

Aboard another steamer heading south about the same time was Fanny Kemble Butler. Fanny was traveling with her husband, an aunt, a maid, and her two children. Sally was three years old and the baby Fan was nine months. Fanny and the children went to the ladies' cabin, while her husband went off, free of cares, to the men's cabin. While Fanny's boat, the *Alabama,* steamed south on Chesapeake Baby, Fanny's main problem was finding towels.

"I had a comical squabble with the stewardess, a good-humored old Negress, who was driven almost wild by my demands for towels," she told her husband. "She assured me that *one* was quite enough."

Fanny had already traveled for hours by the sooty railroad cars to reach the steamboat and had not eaten all day. Her little girl Sally had picked up all the dirty things that only a three-year-old can find, and Fanny wanted to nurse her baby.

"The boat has no less than seven mirrors," Fanny told the stewardess. "And yet there is only one towel for a whole wash-room filled with women and children."

The stewardess finally gave Fanny one towel. When Fanny went into the dressing room to bathe, another lady entered, then went right back out again, apologizing. The stewardess shoved her back toward the door again.

"Go in. Go in," she commanded. "I tell you, they always washes two at a time in them rooms."

While Fanny's journey was to carry her on to her husband's plantation in Georgia, Tyrone Power's trip was one of work. As an actor he was able to play any one of several parts in the most famous plays of the day. Sitting back home in England, he had plotted a course of appearances through the Southlands that he was now finding almost impossible to keep. From South Carolina to Georgia to New Orleans had not looked very far on his map and he imagined that American steamboats and railroads were probably even better and faster than those at home.

Now Power sat on the dock in Columbus, Georgia, wondering how he would ever get to Mobile, Alabama. All the stage-coaches leaving the city the last four days had had accidents. It had been raining for twenty-four hours straight and the roads would be muddier than ever. One man, just returned from the South, told him the last steamboat going down the river had caught fire. All the passengers had swum ashore in their nightclothes and kept alive in a swamp four days before they were rescued. Finally Power settled on a stagecoach to Montgomery, Alabama, and the steamboat *Carolina* down the Alabama River to Mobile.

By the time Power reached the *Carolina*, he was so exhausted from the stagecoach trip that he slept almost twenty-four hours. When he awoke, he found that the boat had moved only fifty miles, because it had stopped at every plantation to pick up muddy, wet bales of cotton. The trip took four days and four nights. Sometimes the fog was so thick they had to tie to a tree along the shore to sleep. Power had plenty of time to record this nonpleasure trip in his journal the Christmas of 1834.

"Occasionally the stream would cant our head suddenly, and before the helm could be shifted, Rush! We went head on into the nearest grove of willows. One man inside the boat was hit by a branch which burst open a side door. There were nearly one hundred on board and each day the boat got smaller because the side galleries were filled in with bales of cotton. The windows were all blocked up and finally only one door was left open. Lights had to be burned in the cabin day and night because no light could get through. We were a floating mass of cotton. If the season had been dry, one unlucky spark might have set us ablaze."

Power enjoyed watching the bales of cotton slide down timber troughs to land at the wharf. At night the slaves who were stationed to keep the great fires going to light up the operation sang, laughed, and yelled confusing directions. When the *Carolina* had finally taken on the last bale it could possibly hold, the water was level with the gunwhales and sloshed over the deck amidships. With a thousand bales on board, the boat still had 150 miles to go. Power thanked heaven their imprisonment would not last much longer.

After playing Mobile and New Orleans, Power boarded another steamboat, the *Superior,* and headed up the Mississippi to Natchez. On this trip he had a little room to himself. Besides a table, chair, and small French bed, it had a window that opened onto the gallery which went around the outside of the boat. Luxury had come to Mississippi River boats that was undreamed of in the East because passengers on these boats often traveled several days at a time.

The lower deck of the *Superior,* where the high-pressure steam boiler and the other machinery were, was used for freight, to store wood for the boiler, and to hold the "deck passengers." These travelers paid only one fourth as much for their passage as those above decks, because they had to cook their own meals and also had to carry the logs on board when the boat stopped twice a day for "wooding."

Memphis, Tennessee, is one of the cities that was built up by steamboat travel along the Mississippi

The other traffic along the river was fascinating to watch. A long square ark flying a white flag turned out to be a floating department store. Several floating sawmills anchored in the river long enough to cut lumber for pioneers who had no other sawmills nearby, then moved on to find work at the next stop. What interested Power most was the floating Mississippi Theater, which was then making its annual voyage downstream. For three or four years the Chapman family had descended the river in a huge flatboat, giving plays that every member of the family appeared in, and sold the theater boat at New Orleans for the price of the wood. They loaded the scenery and costumes on board a steamboat and went back north to build another boat the following year, practice a few new plays, and start all over again. Chapman sounded a trumpet as the barge approached each village or plantation. Usually the troupe was asked to stop, because the villagers knew it would be another year before they would have another chance to see a theater performance.

Steamboats left daily now between the large cities on both the Ohio and Mississippi rivers. Prices, which were very low at first, began rising quickly in 1837. Travelers paid about 2 cents a mile to voyage on the Ohio, but more than double that to go upstream on the Mississippi. The price was still cheap when compared with 6 cents a mile paid for a seat in a stagecoach. Steamboats traveled downstream at about twelve miles an hour, but only half as fast going upstream.

Power had not traveled upstream before, and he was very distressed to find the going so slow. A horse might have moved faster, but Power realized that on land he would not have had the comforts the boat offered. He tried to read, but the boat vibrated so badly he couldn't hold the book still. Every time the boat stopped, he ran down the gangplank to visit with the settlers who lived along the river. Once he asked a settler for a drink of water, then he wasn't sure whether to drink it or not.

"I tell you, sir," said the settler proudly, "there's no pith in any other water after one's been used to drink of *this.*"

He took a long refreshing drink from the cup Power was holding, but Power noticed he did not drink the mud that had settled in the bottom of the cup.

When Power was ready to leave the South in March 1835, he had had enough of the slow struggle of going upstream. Instead, he parted from three of his friends who were taking the steamboat up to Louisville, Kentucky. Power returned to New Orleans to look for a sailing ship. He found one called the *Shakespeare.*

"What's in a name?" Power asked himself and went aboard it on the announced sailing date of Friday, March 20. The boat finally left the wharf on Sunday, which was not surprising to travelers who knew that captains were superstitious about starting a sea voyage on a Friday. A steamboat pulled the *Shakespeare* out to a bar separating the Mississippi River from the Gulf. They were not alone. A British ship, the *Coromandel,* had been stuck on the bar the past forty days.

"Not to worry," the captain told Power. "We shall pass over the bar tomorrow at high tide."

The next afternoon two steamboats, whose business it was to push ships over the bar, made fast to the side of the *Shakespeare.*

"Away we went for a dash at the pass," exclaimed Power, wondering for the third time why he had not taken the steamboat up the Mississippi instead. "The object was to force a ship that draws fifteen feet over a bar that has only twelve feet of water on it. We soon grounded. After a couple of hours tugging, the steamers left us, even though one of the captains said he never quitted a ship that was stuck on the bar."

Three other ships that had left with the *Shakespeare* were

now also stuck fast, in addition to the *Coromandel* that was waiting until the water over the bar was seventeen feet deep —if ever. The two smaller ships managed to slip over the bar on Tuesday, leaving the other ships' passengers to watch them with longing eyes. At long last, late on Wednesday afternoon, the *Shakespeare* slid through the mud and sand. Cheered on by the weary crew of the *Coromandel,* Power sailed off into the Gulf of Mexico.

A Dickens of a Trip

Charles Dickens, author of *Oliver Twist* and *Nicholas Nickleby,* liked his comforts. The steamboats he had seen in England were very comfortable, and he saw no reason why boats in the United States in 1842 should not be just as good.

The first one he sailed on was a small boat going down the Connecticut River to Hartford, Connecticut.

"It is not called a small steamboat without reason. I think it is of about half a pony-power," said Dickens coldly that rainy, January day.

It looked like a little house floating down a river in a flood. The passengers kept to the middle just in case it should tip over. The little house had bright-red curtains and a rocking chair. Dickens laughed.

"It would be impossible to get on anywhere in America without a rocking chair."

Later, after a visit to the nation's capital, Dickens and his wife boarded a steamer that went down the Potomac River.

"It looks like a child's Noah's Ark," he quipped as they went on board the night before sailing so they could get some sleep before the boat left at four in the morning. After leaving his wife in the ladies' cabin, Dickens found the gentlemen's cabin filled with sleepers—all over the floor, tables, berths, chairs,

"Like a mammoth floating bathhouse," said Dickens when he saw his first Mississippi steamboat

and particularly around the hot stove. A steward assigned him a berth that had a curtain around it to give him privacy. But after undressing, he discovered there was no place at all to put his clothes. He laid them tenderly on the floor, knowing very well that it had been spat on thoroughly and that his clothes would have new stains in the morning. Americans all chewed tobacco and not even the carpet of Congress was too good for them to spit on.

At 4 A.M. the boat got under way with so much noise that sleep was impossible. Dickens went into the front cabin washroom. For the use of the fifty passengers, he found two small towels, three small wooden basins, a keg of water and a ladle to put the water into the basin, one six-inch-square mirror, a two-inch piece of yellow soap, one comb, and one brush. A barber was stationed there to shave the gentlemen, but when Dickens used his own comb and brush, a man said he was showing off. He hurried up on deck so as not to miss seeing Mount Vernon as they passed.

"You should see the steamboats on the western rivers," a passenger told him while they were enjoying the view. "You have never seen boats like those anywhere." Dickens decided to look them over.

On Friday, April 1, Dickens was standing on the wharf in Pittsburgh staring up at just such a boat as the stranger had bragged about. He had to admit the man was right. Never had he seen such a steamboat as the *Messenger.*

"So much of American steamboats is out of the water," he mused. This one had no visible deck. There was no mast or rigging. Actually the whole boat looked like a mammoth floating bathhouse with white galleries around it, all resting on top of a barge that was just a few inches above the water. Its engine was completely open to the weather on the lower floor so that one could see the fire in the boiler. Coming out of the top were two iron chimneys, a glass house for the captain, and a safety valve with steam pouring out of it.

Almost thirty years before, Nicholas and Lydia Roosevelt had sailed from this place in the first steamboat down the river. Now Dickens was to follow their course to the Mississippi River in a modern marvel of speed and comfort. Along the white galleries were glass doors, each opening into a private cabin. Inside was one palatial large cabin fitted with rugs, mirrors, and soft chairs. A very long table for dining ran the whole length.

Here breakfast was served at 7 A.M., dinner at 12:30, and a small supper at 6 P.M. Many small dishes were set on the table, "but there was not much food in them," Dickens remarked. His main complaint was not the food, even though the menu consisted of such pioneer delicacies as beetroot, shreds of dried beef, maize, Indian corn, applesauce, pumpkin, beef, pork, and what Dickens referred to as "complicated entanglements of yellow pickles." There was no dinner table conversation. Most travelers from other countries thought Americans ate their meals as if it were a business, never a pleasure. No one shared ideas or traded stories. The manners were even worse than those of the characters Dickens had written into his books. The men spat on the floor and everyone sucked on his fork until he decided what to aim for in the small dishes. Then each plunged that same fork into the serving dishes.

At every turn of the paddle wheels, the steamboat vented a loud, high-pressure blast, "enough to wake up the dead Indians in the mounds." The noise was even louder after the boat entered the Mississippi and began struggling against its strong current. There whole trees floated down the river, torn out of the ground by the spring rains. A lookout on the bow at night rang a bell every time he saw an obstruction.

"That bell is not silent five minutes at a time," Dickens said to his wife. "After every ring there comes a blow which renders it no easy matter to remain in bed."

After the easy trip down the Ohio, the scenery now seemed barely to move as the boat worked upstream. Traveling against what Dickens called "liquid mud going six miles an hour," the steamboat could not do more than ten miles an hour.

Still, Dickens reminded himself, thinking of the muddy stagecoach rides he had taken recently, even this slow going was probably better than a horse could do.

2
Westward on the Rails

Crash! Smash! Dash!
O'er thy iron track, O cars!
And I would that my pen could write out
The sound of thy many jars.
—*Godey's Lady's Book*, 1861

The Steam Locomotive? Never!

For a few years around 1830 it looked as if the railroad would never move faster than a horse.

"God intended the horse for human transportation," protested staunch New Englanders, who seemed to have a direct line to the Almighty where religious matters were concerned. They did not allow even a horse to carry travelers through their villages on a Sunday, but stopped strangers on that day and forced them to go either to church or to jail.

Americans had heard that in England there were carriages with iron horses to pull them. One English locomotive in 1825 had actually pulled thirty-four carriages with loads that weighed ninety tons. But even that locomotive could not go faster than a horse, because of a law that required a boy, carrying a red flag to ride a horse in front of the engine. Horses had to pull the cars too on rainy days, when the engineers refused to take their engines out for fear they would get rusty.

"Horsedrawn carriages are bound to win out over steam engines," said Thomas Earle, a Philadelphia engineer, "because they cost only a bucket of oats to maintain. With heavy steam engines, we would have to build expensive rails across the country."

No invention ever seemed to have more enemies than the iron horse. Farmers didn't want it because, they said, the locomotives would kill their cows, which now roamed freely across the fields. Besides, they would not be able to sell feed to all the horse owners. The city markets would be so full of other farm products carried there by the trains that they would make no money on what they raised. Carriage makers said they would be out of work, and so did the hostlers, canal-boatmen, teamsters, horse dealers, stagecoach drivers, and innkeepers. The American steam boilermakers were angry because the locomotives were to be imported from England. It looked as if no one wanted railroad engines.

The most frightening warning came from the College of Surgeons in Bavaria.

"If railroads are constructed," said the learned doctors, "they will cause the greatest deterioration in the health of the people. Such rapid movement will cause brain trouble among travelers and vertigo [dizziness] for those who look at the speeding trains. High board fences will have to be built along railroad tracks to prevent these dangers."

In the midst of all this hubbub, a group of Marylanders decided to have a race. Peter Cooper had built a strange-looking engine which he called the *Tom Thumb.*

"The *Tom Thumb* is as good as any of those British-built engines," he claimed. "And what's more, I'll race it against a horse-pulled railroad car to prove it."

The race was held on August 28, 1830, near Relay, Maryland. Hundreds of cheering and jeering spectators came to watch. Unfortunately Cooper's *Tom Thumb* broke down in the middle of the race. The horse won, and that—as far as most of the watchers were concerned—settled the matter of iron horses.

Win or lose in that 1830 race, the United States was growing larger and its people needed some way to move west. Horses could never go faster, but there was a chance that the strange little steam engine could. The *Tom Thumb* was put to work on the Baltimore and Ohio Railroad.

The next big event happened in Charleston, South Carolina. On Christmas Day that year, old-timers were surprised to see how many people were in the city. Ordinarily Charleston was deserted by all the townspeople who had plantations, or who had friends to invite them to the country. No one who was *anybody* ever stayed in the city for the holidays. But this year carriages pulled by high-stepping horses were everywhere in town.

The attraction was another little steam engine called the *Best Friend of Charleston.* Standing with two railroad cars that looked like square boxes on flat trucks, the noisy engine straddled a few miles of track that would someday be extended as far as Augusta, Georgia.

The engineer, wearing a black top hat, shook hands with the men on the platform, then swung up behind the steam boiler. The guests, stockholders, and other dignitaries filed through the doors in the center of the coaches. A brass band played "Hail Columbia," drowning out the excited talk of the townspeople who had gathered to watch.

As the *Best Friend of Charleston* started up, the steam let out a screech. The wheels began turning. A well-known scientist had said that the iron wheels would just spin around uselessly on the iron track, but already the little engine had spoiled that prediction.

The military band redoubled its efforts to drown out the engine's noise as the train gathered a little speed. Two artillerymen fired a cannon that had been mounted on a small truck just behind the engine. The train carried the passengers a few miles down the track, where they all disembarked and gave equal time to a picnic supper, toasts, and speeches. Not a discouraging word was heard that day. The next day regular passenger service began on the country's first train.

Iron Horses Take Over

Within the next years railroads began sprouting and branching like morning-glory vines. The locomotive *John Bull* chuffed along the Mohawk and Hudson tracks in New York, pulling a tender, which held barrels of wood, and cars that had been stagecoach bodies. Another railroad was built at Amboy, New Jersey. There passengers from New York City to Philadelphia boarded cars going south to Bordentown, New Jersey, where they got a steamboat down the Delaware River. The small Ponchartrain Railroad carried visitors to New Orleans through miles of swamp. Another, called the Lexington and Ohio, carried passengers west of the Allegheny Mountains. A train from Philadelphia, pulled by the engine *Old Ironsides,* was able to move thirty miles in one hour. It traveled through the village of Germantown to Norristown.

"The American people are on the verge of madness," said a British newspaper editor when he heard that one railroad was to be built just to connect Philadelphia with New York. "The United States is on its way to certain bankruptcy. The rivers and lakes were highways created by Providence for use and are ample for their purpose."

Some days even Americans wondered if they were verging on madness. The new railroads brought new problems which had no solutions yet. The early iron rails, fastened down into granite sills, had a way of working themselves loose. Wooden sills held the rails down better. Sometimes the pressure of an approaching train caused the rails to curl and force upward

Wooden cars splintered in a crash, and hot coals from the heating stoves fueled instant flames

through a car floor, often with disastrous results. The early cars were held together by chains, and constantly jerked and crashed together. Sparks from the engines ignited the passengers' clothing. One lady complained loudly that her new traveling dress and veil had eighteen holes after a sixteen-mile trip. Travelers began to wear long brown-linen overcoats called dusters over their regular clothes. One night sparks set fire to $50,000 in U.S. bank notes. In the confusion of putting out the fire, all the bank notes disappeared, and no one was ever sure how many had burned and how many were stolen.

Almost every issue of the weekly newspaper reported some terrible railroad accident in the country. Many were caused because people were not used to railroads. One man crossing the track in his sleigh could not believe that the oncoming train would not stop and wait for him. Another had his legs broken because he sat between two railroad cars to avoid the cinders and smoke. Still another lost his head by sticking it out of the window as the train approached a bridge. Many an accident was caused by an impatient conductor who did not want to wait on a siding for an oncoming train to pass. By 1840 some railroad crossings had been marked with a wooden arch and a sign: "When the bell rings, look out for the Locomotive."

One way to avoid accidents was to rig up some sort of signal system. The Frenchtown and Newcastle Line was the first to try. The stationmaster raised a large white ball to signal that a train was on time; a black ball showed the train was late. Engineers soon learned they could make a dangerous sound to alert people by releasing and closing the safety valve on the steam boiler. Many inventors tried to find a way to make the brakes work better.

So far no one had discovered a way to keep the dangerous steam engines from blowing up. One exploded when the boiler ran dry and the engineer poured cold water into the hot tank. The *Best Friend of Charleston* lasted only until June 17, 1831. On that day the engineer had gone to lunch, leaving the fireman in charge. Whether he was sleepy or just wanted peace and quiet was never told, but he got tired of the hissing sound of escaping steam, so he tied down the safety valve. He survived with a broken hip.

W. H. Wilson of Philadelphia was just twenty-one when he had his first ride on a railroad in 1832. He was so excited he hardly slept the night before. As soon as the sun rose, he ran all the way from his home to Belmont, where the railroad began. Someday, but not yet, this railroad was to run from Philadelphia to Columbia, Pennsylvania, on the Susquehanna River. There passengers for the west could board a canalboat and eventually arrive in Pittsburgh, 391 miles away.

In 1832 the Columbia Railroad still had a few kinks to be ironed out. One was a hill at Belmont that was too high for the engine to climb. Horses hauled the passengers from Philadelphia in the railroad cars to Belmont. There the horses were untied and the cars attached by ropes to stationary steam engines that pulled them up the inclined plane. At the top, steam engines were attached for the rest of the trip.

"I met Colonel Long at the head of the inclined plane," Wilson says. "Behind the engine *Greenhawk* was an ordinary platform car with ordinary chairs placed on it for the important passengers."

Wilson eagerly found himself a place to sit on the floor of the car, his long legs dangling over the side. There were no brass bands or speeches on this trip. This trial run was for eighteen miles to the end of the line where the lucky passengers planned to have noon dinner at the Green Tree Hotel.

As the engine started up, the cars jerked together and several chairs fell over. Wilson helped the passengers up off their backs. The engine moved a few miles and stopped. The engineer leaped out, tinkered with something, and the cars moved on another few miles. Then he was out again making more adjustments. Every few miles something went wrong. One problem was easily solved. The engine had run out of fuel.

"We were sent off to gather the rails from the fences nearby," said Wilson.

Finally the hungry passengers arrived at the Green Tree at 4 P.M. to find an angry innkeeper.

"I would not have laid the cloth at this late hour," he grumbled, "but for the historic importance of this occasion."

The engineer confided that they might all have to walk home unless he could find more water to make steam.

"Luckily, we found a good well of water near the track," said Wilson. "We formed a line, passing buckets of water to the engineer."

The trip home was not much faster, but Wilson had worked to build this railroad and he was fiercely proud of it. When they reached Belmont at 9 P.M., he raced home with shining eyes to tell his family of the miracle of railroad travel.

Two years later the Columbia Railroad was finished and Wilson was invited to join the important people who had helped to build it.

"It began and ended by horse," said Wilson, "although the engine *Blackhawk* pulled the cars the rest of the time."

The historic trip began at Columbia on the Susquehanna. Several state representatives came from Harrisburg. In only fifty-five minutes the train reached Lancaster, Pennsylvania, and there the party stayed to celebrate with evening dinners and speeches. The next morning the train, now called the Pennsylvania Railroad, carried the passengers to the inclined plane at Belmont in only eight hours. The steam engine was detached and the cars, filled with celebrating riders, shot down the incline, controlled only by gravity. It was by far the fastest part of the trip. Hostlers attached the horses for the journey into the center of Philadelphia, because the railroad bridge was not yet finished across the Schuylkill River.

"Most of the passengers were riding on top—shouting and whooping the whole way," said Wilson. "For three blocks the cars trundled down one narrow street where the second-story windows were on the level with the tops of the cars.

"Since it was past bedtime, most of the townspeople had retired. The unusual noise drew people to their windows to see what was happening. Many were not in very presentable clothing. Upon being cheered by the fun-loving young men—almost within reach of their hands—they retreated fast."

New Rails and New Problems

One day in 1834, Tyrone Power was being whisked at the rate of twenty miles an hour with four hundred other people over a well-constructed railroad.

"The impossible has been achieved," he said to the man sitting next to him. "I find railroads twining and locomotives hissing like serpents over the whole continent from Maine to Mississippi."

Power was a good-natured sort, the kind of person that a man had to be to travel in this new world. He did not grumble constantly about the primitive condition of American roads or complain that American stagecoaches had leather curtains that were rolled down in rainy weather instead of having sturdy wooden sides like English stagecoaches. He didn't even gripe when the locomotive was "not in condition to do duty" and was replaced by a horse that plodded at eight miles an hour.

On this November day he had "risen with the lark" to board the steamboat to Amboy, New Jersey. All the passengers were pleased to find the locomotives in operation, and they looked forward to a quick ride to Bordentown, where they would board the steamboat to Philadelphia.

"We were calculating our rate of travel at about twenty miles per hour," said Power, "when suddenly an alarm was given from the rear. Loud cries of 'Stop the engine!' came from the windows of every carriage in the train. When the engine finally stopped, the carriages were deserted in a moment.

"What a scene was here to witness. One of the coaches in the

The Old Colony Line from Boston to Fall River, Mass., tried a few English railway carriages with "furnished apartments," but Americans did not like them

rear had broken its axle and overturned. Out of twenty-four persons, only one had escaped unhurt. One was dead, another dying. Five others had fractures more or less serious. A couple of ladies were dreadfully wounded and one of their children had a broken limb. Never were sufferers more patient. A fine young surgeon—I learned later that he had broken three ribs in the accident—did the best he could for those hurt worst."

Power offered his help and was set to work binding up broken limbs using pieces of wood from the wrecked carriage for splints. He helped carry the patients to a sandy bank where they could rest until the train was ready to move on. Three hours later the patients were put in the baggage cars and the train set off slowly for Bordentown. Only then did Power learn that John Quincy Adams, retired President of the United States and then a member of Congress, had been sitting in the carriage just ahead of the one that overturned.

It was late evening before all the patients were taken to a Philadelphia hospital. The next day Power visited the survivors to see how they were.

The new railroad between Philadelphia and New York

opened in 1836. Even in small towns people could see that something great was ahead. One rural businessman learned that lime sold in New York City for 75 cents a bushel. The people in his little town paid only 19 cents for his lime. So he sent bushels of lime to New York, for 12 cents a bushel freight charges, and made a nice profit. At this rate the railroad might make everybody rich.

Travelers read in their hometown newspapers about the big new Astor Hotel that opened in New York on January 21, 1836. The "noble structure" had more than three hundred rooms and a "noble dining hall" for gentlemen that was larger than a baseball diamond is today. The ladies' drawing room held the largest mirror in the United States. The kitchen, on the same level as the dining rooms, had its "butteries" arranged so that one chef could supervise all the workers at once. He cooked vegetables and meats in a modern steam apparatus.

Beneath the kitchen was the most surprising thing of all—a laundry and washroom where clothes could be washed, dried, and ready for use in thirty minutes! This miracle was accomplished by spreading the wet clothes on sawhorses that ran on rails into a steam-heated hot room. In five minutes the clothes were dry. Another steam engine pumped water into the four large water reservoirs that were under the roof. From here the water supplied steam to the kitchen and washrooms, where it cleaned "the knives, forks, boots, and shoes."

The grand entrance to the hotel was flanked with marble columns and paved with marble. Few people in all the United States had ever seen such a grand palace. The office was to the right of the entrance, where most smaller hotels had a bar. But the Astor Hotel did not have a bar. The sitting and sleeping apartments were furnished with black walnut furniture. The best rooms had carpets and many had private parlors connected to the bedrooms. The hotel had 450 locks, no two of which opened with the same key. The owners had employed eighty servants, and had marked all the china, silverware, beds, and sheets with "Astor Hotel." They had spent $90,000 on furnishings; $8,000 on silverware, and $12,000 on plated ware.

With such grandeur waiting only a railroad trip away, many people in small towns were impatient for their chance to welcome a new railroad. The welcoming ceremony was almost always the same.

First, something had to be carried to celebrate a "wedding." In Florida it was the waters of Lake DeSoto and of the St. John's River that were mingled. The Western Railroad (later called Boston and Albany) opened by delivering to Albany candles made that morning of whale oil in New Bedford, and to Boston table salt that had been the day before in a mine near Syracuse, New York. No celebration was official without plenty of good food, often shared by uninvited spectators, because the trays loaded with goodies were carried through the crowd to the invited guests. The master of ceremonies always offered a toast to the health of the guests. Then anyone who felt inspired could jump up, glass in hand, and propose a toast to someone else. This person, having been toasted, must then have a response ready. Any person who did not respond to a toast set a bad example in not performing his social obligations. After hours of toasting and speechmaking came the high point—a ride on the new railroad.

Not all new railroad celebrations turned out as scheduled, however. The managers of a new railroad between Reading and Pottstown, Pennsylvania, decided to have a gala opening in December of 1837, even though their railroad was not quite finished. Their passenger engine *Delaware* had just been fished out of the Delaware River where it had fallen while being loaded onto a canalboat. The celebrants were ready for the great occasion to begin when the engineer noticed that the *Delaware* had been made too wide or else the tracks were too narrow. Quickly the engineers rounded up as many stagecoach horses as they could find and attached them to the cars instead. The band played and the militia shot off their flintlocks as the first "train" pulled out of Reading with the mayor, town council, and important guests aboard. Soon the train reached a trestle over a stream, but there were no floorboards on the trestle. The horses refused to walk on the crossties. So the mayor, town council, and guests pushed the cars over the bridge while the horses were led down and around it and attached again on the other side. The group finally arrived in Pottstown and were entertained a little too well. Most were feeling boisterous when it came time for the return trip. One coach and its horses fell down a bank, but no one was injured, and most of the guests made it home that night.

Most railroad celebrations ended with the start of regular railroad service the next day. Then ordinary people had their chance to ride. They bought their tickets in a shop or grocery from the train's conductor since most towns had no depots yet. The gentlemen shook hands with the top-hatted and frock-coated engineer before they boarded the train. Ladies were always greeted by the engineer, who assured them that sitting in the railroad train now was as safe as sitting in their own parlors.

One of the biggest problems for the first railroad passengers was telling the time. The country had no standard time yet, and time was reckoned by the sun's passage. In Reading, Pennsylvania, about sixty miles west of Philadelphia, the time was fifteen minutes later than in the city. Just as in many other towns in the United States, the residents of Reading depended on the church bell to tell them when it was 8 A.M. and midnight. They set their clocks twice a day by that bell. But the railroad, running on Philadelphia time, left fifteen minutes before the passengers arrived at the platform. Most towns found it simpler to change their own times. From then on, businesses and schools ran on "railroad time."

The railroad made much more difference in people's lives than they had thought possible. The people in Reading, for instance, remembered when their parents' trips to Philadelphia had taken thirty-one hours by stagecoach. On the railroad, the same trip took three hours.

By 1835, New England, where God had intended the horse for human transportation, had more railroads than any other part of the country. By that summer, a traveler could eat his noon meal in Boston and board the train to Providence, Rhode Island. At four he boarded a steamboat and arrived in New York the next morning. It was a miracle.

Comforts on the Railroad

"I wish I had eaten lunch," Harriet Martineau groaned as she got out of a stagecoach one March day in 1837. She had missed the train and so had taken the coach to a place called Branchville, where, the driver assured her, she could catch the same train at noon. The train, as he predicted, was two hours late.

"But I'll be in Charleston in three or four hours at the most," Harriet consoled herself. "Then I'll have a first-rate supper."

The train plodded through swampy land at fourteen miles an hour. At four thirty the boiler sprang a leak, and the passengers had to sit two hours while the engineer and fireman patched it. Again and again it broke down, always, it seemed, in the middle of a swamp. The ladies dared not leave the cars, but the gentlemen stretched their legs and amused themselves trying to catch frogs. Once the train broke down in front of a house where, Harriet says, the travelers could see a hot supper actually being set on the table.

"The men ran into the house and gave the people money for their food. One man got a whole chicken. One brought back part of a turkey. My gentleman was not alert enough. He brought back strips of ham, pieces of dried bread, and three sweet potatoes all jumbled together in his handkerchief."

The food helped the passengers survive, which was just as well, because the engine never stopped breaking down. An hour later they were stuck in the middle of another swamp. The passengers fell asleep from exhaustion.

"We were awakened by such a din as I never heard," said Harriet, who could not remember at first where she was. "The noise was a frog concert from yet another swamp where the train had stopped." The train finally arrived in Charleston at 4:30 A.M.

Another woman traveler was actress Fanny Kemble Butler. When she heard there were two routes to Baltimore from Philadelphia, she chose the shortest—by railroad. She was traveling with her husband, an aunt, a maid named Margery, and two little children. The railroad sounded so much easier—no changing from steamboat to train to steamboat again. The Butler family left Philadelphia at daybreak on Friday, December 21, 1838.

"The heat inside the ladies' carriage was terrible."

Fanny, like most English people, would rather have dressed in layers of warm clothing and dispensed with the glowing stove that burned coal and sent off "poison fumes." At least the air would have smelled better without heat. The other passengers complained when she tried to open a window, so she sat down next to her aunt and tried not to breathe deeply. The seats were "a pretty tight fit" for the ladies in their traveling dresses. Fanny put three-year-old Sally to sleep on the opposite seat, but the train's jolting kept bouncing the little girl off the seat.

"A whole tribe of little itinerant fruit and cake sellers rushed through the car every time the train stopped."

Fanny could not bear to eat what they sold because the sellers all looked so dirty. She was disgusted with the way other mothers on the train stuffed their children on the trip to keep them quiet. One offered a piece of pound cake to Sally.

"No, thank you," said Fanny firmly, before her daughter could take the cake.

"It helps to keep the babies good," argued the other mother. "Don't you allow her to eat cake?"

"She eats only bread, milk, and meat," said Fanny.

"No tea or coffee?" asked the mother, her eyes wide. "No butter?"

"None," said Fanny, in a tone of voice that made the lady back off with a pitying glance at little Sally. The lady told someone later that Fanny "put on airs. She even bathes her children on the train! Fancy that."

Fanny nursed her baby, Fan, glad to have the privacy of a railroad coach with only ladies in it. However, she thought as the train barreled along, it was too bad that the men were always shunted off to another coach. This strange custom deprived her of her husband's companionship and also left the ladies with the sole care of the children. At the same time, her husband was not enjoying his ride in the men's coach. Most of the men either smoked cigars or chewed tobacco and spit on the floor. Little did Fanny dream that this train was to be followed by far worse trains.

"Our train from Portsmouth, Virginia, to Weldon, North Carolina, was a kettle," Fanny observed. This was her first day in the Deep South and the sight of Negro slaves had upset her badly. At one small village, the Negroes had gathered in crowds to stare at the strangers on the train. Little Sally leaned from the window to wave to them. One lady held up her little black child of about the same age.

"A waiting maid for the little missis," said the black mother.

Fanny was shocked. Was the black mother serious? Was she really offering her child—perhaps hoping the child would have a better life?

"The little missis waits on herself," Fanny answered.

The black mothers all giggled at this. Later Fanny learned that no southern ladies waited on themselves. She was entering a frightening new life. When she had married her husband, Pierce Butler, he did not own a plantation with Negro slaves. He had only just inherited it. Now they were on their way to Georgia, and already Fanny knew in her heart that she would not be able to endure this slavery business. She looked at her sleeping children, and the train entered another swamp. Instinctively she leaned over and covered Sally's and Fan's noses with clean handkerchiefs. She was afraid that even going through the swamp as fast as the train moved might make them sick with its "stagnant waters and poisonous vegetation."

When the train stopped at Weldon, Fanny found that it was not a place, but "the place where a place was intended to be."

Weldon had only a few miserable rough pine buildings. Fanny was not sure whether they were half built up or not quite fallen down. One very dirty-looking old wooden house turned out to be the inn where they were to have dinner and wait for another train to take them farther south.

"The women were shown up a filthy flight of wooden stairs into a dilapidated room. The plastered walls were all smeared and discolored. Three beds were in the room strewn with tattered articles of male and female apparel. Then we were called to dinner.

"Everything looked so dirty. The chickens were so tough

Fanny wondered what was ahead for her in Georgia
when she saw this railroad station

that I should think they must have been alive when we came into the house and certainly had died very hard." Fanny was glad she didn't know what the black matter was that the chickens were stuffed with.

At eight thirty that night the branch train arrived, and Fanny could share a compartment with her husband. They had just fallen asleep when the train stopped at midnight. The conductor announced it was the end of the line. From here they crowded into a stagecoach to reach the next railroad line, miles away. The bridge across the Neuse River was so shaky that the stagecoach passengers had to get out and walk across it in the rain. When they finally reached the other railroad, the train had not arrived. There was not a sign of a house or an inn.

There were plenty of people, however. They had all collected to see the "hot-water carriages" because this was only the third day the railroad had been operating. It was getting dark when one of the people remembered that a Colonel lived nearby on a plantation. The women and children climbed onto an empty flatbed car and several black men pushed it along the track toward the Colonel's farm. Across the deep ravines the iron road was not finished—only the rails crossed on pilings. At about five they reached a primitive building—not at all the plantation house Fanny had imagined. The old Colonel sat before a huge pinewood fire and ordered his tribe of slaves to get food for the strangers. The wind whistled through the planks and broken windows, so the ladies hung their cloaks and shawls over the leaks to keep some warmth inside.

Looking around after they sat down, Fanny began wondering what was ahead for her family at her husband's Georgia plantation. Did it look like this brick-and-plank house with not even a touch of plaster to the walls? In the corner was a bed, an old case clock, and chairs of several shapes and sizes. The walls were decorated with turkey feather fans, medicine bottles, bunches of dried herbs, and old guns. Dinner, when it came, consisted of dirty water called tea, old cheese, bad butter, and old dry biscuits. When the train finally arrived at 8 P.M. the Colonel charged each of them 50 cents for his hospitality.

They were to arrive at Wilmington, North Carolina, in five hours, but they jolted on and on. The carriage stove poured out clouds of smoke every time new coals were added. The train finally stopped and the conductor woke those passengers who had been lucky enough to fall asleep.

"It was 5 A.M.—dark, and bitter cold," said Fanny. The nearest inn, said the conductor, was over a mile away and there was no way to get there except to walk along the edge of the Cape Fear River without any lantern.

"When we finally arrived at an inn, I asked for tea." Fanny had not eaten all day, except for some food lumps at the Colonel's that she had hardly been able to swallow.

"The public breakfast will not be ready for some hours yet," said the landlord coldly.

He made no move to satisfy any of their requests, but showed them to a room without curtains or shutters, and with windows that could not be closed.

"There are not enough beds," Fanny said, after a look.

"This is the only room we have. Take it or leave it."

After three sleepless nights, Fanny and the others could probably have slept standing straight up. Margery, the maid, slept with the two children. Aunty lay on a curtainless cot in the corner. Fanny stretched out on a mattress on the floor. She had just closed her eyes, it seemed, when an alarm bell rang. Breakfast was served.

"No matter how hungry you arrive at an inn, you can't eat until those who are not starving desire to eat," she moaned. Turning over, she fell asleep again.

Railroads were no longer new by the time Charles Godfrey Leland rode from Philadelphia to Baltimore at the end of October 1847. He liked knowing that trains were now modern, and he looked forward to a comfortable ride, unlike those his friends had talked about.

"I left Philadelphia on Friday evening at 10 P.M. in the cars from Eleventh and Market streets, and secured a seat as close to the stove as a human body could stand. At Gray's Ferry the iron horse was attached and I settled myself for a comfortable sleep.

"Vain hope! The seats are double with something between —just a board—nothing to rest the arm on. I had the misfortune to have a 'rum-un' on the seat next me. Compound smells issued from him like a bar, smoking room, circus, third tier, or gas factory—odors highly flavored with peach brandy. My only way was to turn my back on him. Thank God he got off in

Wilmington." Leland drew his first deep breath.

When the train arrived at Havre de Grace, Maryland, the passengers all got out and crossed the Susquehanna River in a ferryboat. In half an hour they had boarded the railroad cars on the other side and started off again.

The moon shone out clear and silvery on woodland and meadow, and Leland was on that happy point, just cheating himself into the belief of a little sleep, when the cars came to a dead halt. One or two nervous persons wandered out, leaving the car door open, to see the "doings of the outsiders." They came back in to report the train was waiting for another one to pass.

An old gentleman piped up: "Is it possible there is only one track on this road?" He put this question in a general manner to the whole car. Silence. Then a man in one corner, away from the stove and cold, replied, "Only one." Old gentleman: "Very dangerous way. They might meet."

"Reckon they do at times. Came through sometime sence and just beyont hyar we turned a corna and struck tother line smack!"

"Anyone hurt?" asked the old gentleman.

"Not a man. But the way we made the splinters fly was a caution. Wuss than Kilkenny cats!"

He had scarcely finished speaking when, *Rattle . . . dash . . . thum . . . dash . . . plunk,* and all the cars struck together. *Wherrrr . . . whoooo . . . uuu . . .* and the cars were again in motion. Conversation dropped into a lower key. Someone piled more wood into the stove. It grew warmer, and was becoming lighter. Fences and trees loomed out stronger. Moonlight was giving way to day-dawn, when *jerk!* Motion stopped.

"Out go the nervous," wrote Leland in his diary, "report frost on track and engine weak. Can't move on the rail. Under way again. Another stop. Same cause. One or two passengers 'loud up.'

"*Wherrr . . . herrr . . . herrr . . .* Round go the engine wheels but can't hold. More delay. Some strong interjections used by crowd inside . . . a bad word used often, applied to company and cars, not forgetting the cause, the frost.

"Started at last and made good time, till . . . *Rattle . . .* turn . . . turn . . . and we are again at a standstill.

" 'Damn this work,' say some. 'Why don't they have better engines?'

"Then all was quiet. Found that the engine, with the mail-bags and baggage, had started for Baltimore and left the cars with passengers, fearful that the line would be too late to catch the southern mail.

"There was such a hailstorm of abuse as was showered down when the insiders found out how the outsiders had left them in the lurch. If curses loud and deep were any go, the souls of some of the managers of the line stood about as good a chance of seeing heaven as one's old shoes.

"Well, to sum up, we were five hours traveling forty miles from the river to Baltimore—a horse could have done better."

Long Distance Railroads

Short local railroad lines soon joined to make longer lines, reaching like fingers toward the West. Settlers who wanted to go where land was cheap dreamed of a railroad they could get on and not get off until they were there.

People in New York State had planned for just such a railroad in 1832, when Colonel DeWitt Clinton, Jr., surveyed the land from Albany to Lake Erie. But when the railroad was mentioned in the state legislature, protestors argued.

"The idea is impracticable and useless," said some.

"Such a railroad could *never* be made," said others. "And even if it were, it would never be used because the land out there is mountainous and worthless. There would be no products to send to market."

In 1841 a railroad reached from New England to Albany. The time had come to continue that railroad through New York State. Within ten years the "Lion of Railways" (the New York and Lake Erie) was almost finished, but passengers could not board the train at Albany. Tourists from New England took stagecoaches to get on the train at a stop farther west.

Passengers from New York City took the Hudson River steamboat northward to a new place called Piermont. Gentlemen boarded the steamboat in New York City in the morning, had a leisurely breakfast, smoked a cigar, and read the morning newspaper. Eager young travelers watched for the bright yellow pier, almost a mile long, that extended out into the river. When they reached Piermont, across the river from Tarrytown, they walked down the wide wharf toward the land. The more curious peeked inside the huge buildings where all the freight and baggage were stored and passenger cars for the railroad were built. Here the cars were repaired, painted, and upholstered. The engine house had space for twenty-eight engines. The company was proud of its T-rails, designed to "give a remarkably easy and steady motion to the cars." The cars were wide and luxurious inside. No one had ever ridden in a train like this one.

As the people from the steamboats boarded the train, the steam whistle blew. Most train whistles were shrill and hurt the eardrums. But the one on "The Lion of Railways" had a hoarse sound.

"A churchyard sound," the passengers called it, because a person whose voice sounded like that would soon be "six feet under" in the church graveyard.

As the train started up a steep grade, the passengers were quiet with apprehension. The grade was four times as steep as those the first railroad engines could climb, but the "Lion" made it easily. The first sixty miles of the trip was called the "Milky Way," because the platforms along the tracks were filled with milk cans. Heading north, the train delivered empty cans. Heading south, the train picked up filled cans to be delivered in New York City early in the morning. At Monroe, fifty miles out of New York, farmers loaded two hundred milk cans, each one holding fifteen gallons, every day. The dealers bought the milk for two cents a quart.

One of the "lions" to watch for along the New York & Lake Erie Railroad was this hill shaped like "Anthony's Nose"

The railroad company published its own railroad guide for passengers, just as the steamboat companies had. But the writers did little to stir up interest in the passing scenery. While the steamboat guides described all the exciting and well-known sights, along with facts and figures to tell the folks at home later, the railroad guide was probably too honest.

"Nothing more may be said of Spring Valley and Monsey than they are a pair of uninteresting settlements growing up around the stations, placed in a dull-looking country," the guidebook said on one page. And on another, "Four miles of the descent from Summit are as stupid as can possibly be, because the view is shut in by woods."

At the village of Suffern, the train became more crowded as passengers from Jersey City left the small-gage Union Railroad there to ride in more luxury on the New York and Lake Erie. Beyond Suffern the railroad crossed a marshy flat. Travelers held their breath while the heavy train lumbered and swayed across a bridge built on pilings driven into the swamp. City people perked up when the train passed the village of Goshen. They had heard of Goshen milk and butter, and this was where it came from.

As the train rolled into wilder country, hunters and other sportsmen signaled to the conductor to let them off. Occasionally a hunter with his trophies slung over his shoulder signaled for the train to stop and pick him up. At Narrowsburgh was a summer boardinghouse. Several families left the train there for a vacation. The rest of the passengers got off to go into the refreshment room. They had only ten minutes to buy their food, pay for it, and eat it. Most people gave up trying to eat in refreshment rooms and just carried gingerbread to nibble instead. Those with the loudest voices and the longest arms were the only ones who succeeded in buying food.

The best view of the entire trip was at Summit. There one

lucky passenger bribed the engineer into sharing his seat so the passenger could enjoy the best view. Summit was so high that an enginehouse and a turnout stood by with a reserve engine just in case one was needed. Snow often drifted deeply there, making the trip in winter dangerous and slow.

One passenger on the train remembered making this same trip in the years before the railroad. Although the stagecoaches he had ridden in were supposed to travel seven miles an hour, few of them ever hit top speed. The road was cut into broad and deep gullies. Rain had poured against the coach's leather

Ten minutes to eat—and then it was "All Aboard" again

Emigrants heading west had to mark their baggage clearly and watch it carefully until it was loaded onto the train

curtains and down into his lap. One day of the trip, he and three other men had rented "an extra" for $75.

"The driver charged over corduroy roads," he told the train passengers. "Only he called it the Canadian railway. He shouted to us tumbling about inside: 'Look out now, not to get mixed up of a heap!' I tell you that road coming into Buffalo was so terrible that any man with loose teeth would do better to walk the distance."

In 1850, the New York and Lake Erie ran just beyond Elmira, New York, not very near the lake. The passengers had to take a crowded stagecoach from there, but they had tasted progress. Never again would a horse look as good as it used to. Soon the cars ran all the way to the lake and the tourists could board a lake steamboat and head toward the sunset. Another doorway to the West had been opened.

Ho! for "Kanzas" and Points West

"The office of the New England Emigrant Aid Company will *not* pay the expenses in transporting individuals to Kanzas," said the brochure, "but it will arrange a cheaper fare."

Thousands of New Englanders read the advertisement in 1856 and began packing their belongings. The time to travel in luxury had come. Even their wives agreed that the trip held no fears now that the railroad went west. Every week, starting

Men slept in three tiers on the New York Central sleeping car

in March when the ice had melted on the rivers and Great Lakes, the New England Emigrant Aid Company formed parties of up to one hundred settlers to travel west. They were called "emigrants" because the western lands where they were going were actually outside the United States at first. That new land could not be turned into states until enough people lived there to send representatives to Congress.

"Those going early will have more annoyances," the Emigrant Aid Company admitted, "but they will have a better choice of land."

The cost to each adult was about forty dollars, starting from Boston, where the railroad began. Children between four and twelve were half price, and those under four were free. The earliest parties traveled most of the way to St. Louis by railroad, but as soon as Lake Erie navigation opened in the spring, that route was preferred. The price included meals and lodging between St. Louis and Kanzas City. To travel the "old" way —by covered wagon—an emigrant would have had to pay fifty dollars just for a pair of oxen, and then the trip would have taken two or three months. By the railroad, traveling day and night, with no worries about the weather, the settler's trip took a few weeks. When the railroad was finished farther west, the trip would take only a few days.

Late the first night, the emigrants reached Albany, where lodging and breakfast cost 75 cents each. From there they took the Erie Canal to Buffalo or traveled by steamboat to Piermont, where they boarded the train.

Each traveler was allowed one hundred pounds of baggage, packed in trunks, chests, or very well made boxes with strong handles. He wrote "Kanzas Party's Baggage" on the side of each piece, along with his own name and destination.

The company advised the emigrants to take sturdy clothing, "suitable for service, not show," and their bedding. Mechanics who needed their tools with them found their own baggage reached the hundred-pound limit very fast. They shipped their furniture by freight and planned to buy the basic necessities for housekeeping or farming after they reached St. Louis. They could buy cows for about $25, a yoke of oxen for $50 to $100, horses for about $75, and sheep for $2 each after they reached Kanzas.

The company said an industrious and healthy person needed only one hundred dollars clear to keep from hunger. A United States citizen, a widow, or a single man over twenty-one could buy land from the government for $1.25 an acre, with a limit of 160 acres. The buyer paid for the land after a government survey was completed or just before the public land sale in a particular area.

After reaching Kanzas City, the emigrants were on their own. There were no hotels, and the only places they could buy the simplest supplies were at Leavenworth and Lawrence in Kanzas. Some of the settlers headed farther up the Missouri River into Nebraska and the Dakota country. Others went west, looking for farmland to buy.

"If you have a large family," the Emigrant Aid Company warned, "take along a boiled ham in a tin can or some corned beef, crackers, and cheese. At St. Louis you can buy a canteen, gourd, leather tank, or other water holder that is not easily broken. At most of the boat landings you can find fresh springwater, so you will not need to drink the Missouri River water —a great cause of the bowel complaints among travelers in that region."

The company's guidebook tried hard to prepare the pioneers for what was ahead, but avoided saying something that might be downright discouraging. There was the matter of building a house, for example. Instead of telling the settlers that there was no way they could build a log cabin because there were no trees, the book just said "there is no oversupply of timber" and told them how much faster the farmer could plow with no trees in the way. The timber was "temporarily short" because of the great prairie fires, but the Emigrant Aid Company was sure there would be many woodlands in Kanzas as soon as several people settled there. The many cottonwood trees that grew along the edges of streams turned out to be useless to builders. The cottonwood could not be planed. If it was used for fences, the posts rotted in the ground, and when it was nailed onto a wall, the wood warped and broke away from the nails. Meanwhile there was enough lime and clay to build walls for a house. A small stone house would cost more —from $350 up. Settlers could make fences by planting thorny Osage orange hedges to enclose their animals.

The weather was another question in the settlers' minds. What was it like? The company told them that the snow was never deeper than six inches, and a man could work without putting on a coat until the end of December. The rainfall was less than thirty inches a year. As for summer, in the hottest month of July the temperature rose to almost 100° "with gentle cooling winds."

The company did not guarantee a job for the settlers, but it did encourage men with a trade like carpentry, masonry, blacksmithing, harnessmaking, or brickmaking to pack up and join the group. Laborers earned $1.50 a day and carpenters $2.50 in the West. Farmers had to pay $3 an acre to have their land broken the first year. Most farmers got together, helping one another, to save money and time.

The company said the emigrants had nothing to fear from the Indians, "because the Shawnees, Wyandots, and Delawares were almost civilized compared to the roving wild Indians of other western areas." The pioneers had only to "live by the Golden Rule," and they would get along fine. However, they should bring along their guns. The area was full of deer, squirrels, ducks, turkeys, and even buffalo. And there was always the chance they might run into one of the "rare bands of Indians from the Rocky Mountains."

Railroad to the Mississippi

On Monday, June 1, 1857, thousands of people were milling around the Baltimore and Ohio Railroad station. Captain George Rawlings, the conductor in charge of the train, thought he had seen the largest crowd in his life in March when 8,000 people swarmed into Washington City, to see James Buchanan sworn in as President. Now the excited passengers who crowded into the cars at 6 A.M. barely found room to sit down.

"All aboard!" the conductor shouted as the whistle shrieked. Thousands of spectators cheered. The Independent Blues, Baltimore's military band, played a march as they filed into one of the coaches. Two heavy locomotives strained and let off steam as the wheels began to turn. The first passenger train from Baltimore to St. Louis on the Mississippi River was on its way. Only a generation ago the river had been called "the West Coast." Now everyone knew there was another West Coast, and someday the railroad would run all the way to that far shore.

At Washington Junction a full train from Washington and Annapolis spilled out its passengers, who wedged their way into the crowded cars. Among them was the Honorable Lewis Cass, Secretary of State and a former general. In spite of rain, everyone was in the best of spirits and the tourists chatted happily with each other. The old custom of never speaking to anyone "in a public place" was forgotten—at least for this trip. When the train crossed an iron bridge, everyone piled out to see this modern wonder. When it was built, engineers had thought no iron bridge could be as strong as one of wood or stone.

At Harper's Ferry, in what is now West Virginia, sixty more people squeezed into the bulging cars.

The train stopped at Grafton, West Virginia, at nine for the passengers to sleep in local homes and hotels. But sleep did not come soon. Thousands of villagers and other people who had traveled miles to see the train had built a huge bonfire. The local artillery fired salvos every few minutes. Another train-load of passengers arrived to join the excursion, making it almost impossible to find a place to lie down for the night. Some bedded in the railroad cars, although the band playing and the people milling around to admire the cars made sleep difficult.

Long before sunrise, the travelers were awake to sightsee the village and stretch their legs. By six they had eaten breakfast and hurried back to find seats on the train. The train tracks led through 23 tunnels and between heavy embankments, so there was not much to see.

"The morning's journey led us to believe we had discovered the Underground Railroad at last," joked one man.

At every crossroads along the way, people stood waving handkerchiefs and cheering. Every community that could form a band placed it alongside the track, playing for all it was worth, as the train whizzed by at a marvelous twenty miles an hour.

On Wednesday, June 3, the easterners left Chillicothe, Ohio, at 9 A.M. for the final run to Cincinnati. There were now 2,500 persons, filling several trains. Part of the road had not been ballasted yet, but the passengers were more than willing to put up with minor bumping and jouncing. They arrived at the end of the line in the "Queen City of the West" at 1 P.M. Across the city was another track to the west. Engines and cars had steamed in from St. Louis bringing another thousand people.

The eastward-bound travelers from St. Louis had arrived the day before, so the crowd that greeted the westward-bound train's arrival was larger than anyone in the Midwest had ever seen. The mayor stood on the platform, flanked by two corps of militia, ready to make yet another speech. Then the crowd escorted the new arrivals to Burnet House, where the ceremonial speechmaking began. Speeches were such an important part of these occasions that the crowd booed when the Secretary of State, General Lewis Cass, refused to make an oration.

"The heat and dust and confusion of a railroad car are bad preparations for a speech," he apologized, touching a nerve of the railroad managers, who thought he should be praising their railroad, not complaining about it.

Not all the arrivals stayed for the speeches. With over 20,000 strangers in town, the search for a bed had to begin at once.

"Hotel rooms are scarce as money in a bank panic," one man commented. Luckily, many Cincinnati citizens invited strangers into their homes. Some found space in the steamboats. Cincinnati was almost buried in flags, banners, festoons of evergreens, floral wreaths, and "quaint devices" made of flowers. Mottoes hung from roofs and windows.

"The iron track is the only true bond of Union," was tacked over the railroad store. Everywhere were smaller signs saying "Baltimore . . . Cincinnati . . . and St. Louis" and "Cincinnati sends Greetings East and West." Another large sign read "A Locomotive is the only good Motive—for Riding a Man on a Rail." The *Times* newspaper building was almost hidden behind a huge illustration showing a locomotive whizzing over a track in hot pursuit of an Indian on a pony. Another painting, more than thirty feet long, showed the West in 1807 with a pioneer and his cabin, and the West in 1857 with a large city, a train, and a suspension bridge over the Ohio River. One of the cleverest displays was at John Hise's trunk manufacturing company, where someone had made a locomotive out of several sizes of trunks, labeling it "The Great Trunk Railway."

The special feature of the holiday was a grand demonstration of steam fire engines. At 4 P.M. the fire bell sounded and every engine, ladder, and hose carriage raced to the large open space at the Fifth Street Market. The engines, each pulled by four powerful horses, looked fierce with heavy black smoke pouring from their chimneys. The firemen were all screaming challenges at each other, because it was a race between rival companies. Within one minute, the firemen had set up the ladders, even on the tallest buildings, which were five stories high. Three minutes later came the hose carriages, unreeling hoses as they came. In four minutes the first water had been turned on and reached as high as five stories. In less than six minutes the steam was up, and six more engines threw streams of water. Each new jet of water brought shouts of approval from the crowd.

Secretary of State Cass, who had not been able to see well enough from his carriage, had the driver move closer to the action. Suddenly a stream of water was turned in his direction and "showered the general's party plentifully." Cass stood up to let the water run off and smiled stiffly to the laughing crowd.

The demonstration ended with the firemen bringing together seven streams of water and fastening the hoses in a frame. The jets sprayed one hundred feet into the sky. The center stream shot almost twice as high, and rainbows played around the display.

Later the visitors toured the city. In the evening came more speeches and brass bands, while travelers who dreaded the crowds that would be leaving the next day boarded a night train to St. Louis. They missed the dinner parties and the tables decorated with railroad engines, stations, and cars made of spun sugar. Five hundred people went to a fashionable ball at Burnet House and danced until midnight, when supper was served in the great hall.

The next morning there were not enough coaches to hold all the people who wanted to go on to St. Louis. Over 1,500 people crowded into the eighteen passenger cars pulled by two separate engines. The rear car of the first train carried the families of the railroad directors. This special car was "something new in the history of railroad travel." It had four elegantly painted compartments, each with sofas that turned into double beds at night, and several richly upholstered chairs. The car also had a "heating furnace" that brought in cool breezes without dust on a summer day. As the trains left for St. Louis from the station in west Cincinnati, other trains left for Baltimore from the east Cincinnati station.

The first westbound engine hadn't moved sixteen miles before the pumps gave out and had to be repaired. The tourists had been so used to repairs along the road when they traveled by stagecoach that the delay hardly bothered them. They piled out of the cars and went sightseeing. The home of General William H. Harrison, who was known as "Old Tip" since the Battle of Tippecanoe, was nearby. His widow was somewhat shocked to see a group of 800 people suddenly paying a call to her husband's tomb early that morning.

Boarding again, the jolly crowd waved back happily to the men, women, and children waving wildly beside the tracks. Every so often the train passed spare engines, chugging away on sidings with their steam up, all ready to go if they should be needed. Refreshments served in the cars included cold chicken, ice cream, and sparkling catawba wine. The good food helped make up for the scarcity of scenery. Only where a road crossed the tracks could the passengers see beyond the trees. About six hours after leaving Cincinnati, the train pulled off onto a siding and stopped for food at an unfinished station house at Fort Ritner, Indiana.

"Eight hundred passengers charged the fort," said one hungry passenger. There was only enough food for 150 people.

A second train overtook the first train there and raced on to Vincennes, Indiana, three hours away. Here was a sort of "halfway house," one day to become a station. The ladies of the town had prepared a nice meal, setting the tables under the trees. But a heavy rain had begun just before the trains arrived, and the women had to hurry the tables under a temporary shed. The passengers from both trains tried to eat while the townspeople carried out their preplanned program with greetings, toasts, and wordy speeches. When the train whistles blew, each train had two new locomotives for the eight-hour dash to St. Louis.

One train broke down just after Vincennes where there was no siding, and that ended the racing competition. The passengers entertained themselves with speeches until the whistle blew and they were off once more, rushing across the flat plains of Illinois. As it grew dark, the trains passed houses with windows illuminated by candles. Those who had no candles set fire to tar barrels. These were not the brilliant "illuminations" that easterners were used to seeing on special occasions in their cities, but here in the pitch-black countryside, the small lights were just as effective, bringing tears to some eyes. The message was one of shared excitement that at last the railroad was coming through. Every homesick settler was saying, "I no longer have to feel that I will never see my family again. . . . The railroad track goes all the way back to my home, and I can see home again before I die."

Close to midnight, just as passengers were dozing off into dreams of the past night's celebrations, someone by a window shouted.

"Look, pine torches!"

All along the railroad, bright-burning torches lighted up the way. Soon cannons were booming. The Mississippi River lay just ahead—and across the water was St. Louis, the new Gateway to the West. As the trains slowed and finally stopped, many were too sleepy to hear yet another speech, from the mayor of St. Louis.

"We stand upon that machine," said the mayor to his drowsy audience, "that is to make the crooked places straight, the rough places smooth, and the wilderness as a garden."

He was mercifully brief, and the travelers carried their baggage toward four elegant Mississippi River steamboats: the *Reindeer,* the *Baltimore,* the *Illinois,* and *Die Vernon.* After changing their dusty clothing in the steamboat staterooms, they sat down to a huge supper. The great hall of each steamboat filled the entire center, three tiers high. Across the river, even though it was long after midnight, fireworks shot into the black western sky. The entire shore was lighted by torches, Roman candles, and Grecian fire. The next morning, after breakfast on the steamboats and a short trip upriver to see the western shore, there were to be two days of parties.

Transcontinental at Last

"The Eastern half of the United States doesn't begin to prepare you for the Western half," the early emigrants wrote back home.

So many things were different they hardly knew where to begin. The manure that farmers used to fertilize fields in the East just dried up and blew away in western states. The "cooling breezes" of the plains sometimes blew for days with the violence of a hurricane. In dry weather the same winds could spread fires that wiped out a man's farm, livestock, and home in seconds. For years people had built their homes in one area of Denver, until one day "a full-blown river marched abreast with torrent force" and washed everything away. After that, western people respected dry riverbeds. Even the Rocky Mountains were not like other mountains. They were much higher than the White Mountains of New Hampshire, where vegetation slowed down at 5,000 feet. In the Rockies, the hills began at that altitude, and some of the best trees were found at 11,000 feet.

In 1865, emigrants traveled beyond the Missouri River toward the Rocky Mountains by stagecoach. Their ride took six days and six nights. The drivers stopped every ten or twelve miles to change horses and every forty or fifty miles to eat. Now, only three years later, the same trip by railroad was measured by hours.

"We felt perfectly safe from Indians in the swiftly moving

"We felt perfectly safe from Indians," said one emigrant wife of the train

train," one pioneer's wife told her parents back East. "The car was an elegant drawing room by day and a luxurious bedroom at night. One car, the Pullman Palace, even had an organ and we gathered around it for hours singing songs of home."

In 1866, Omaha, Nebraska, was a small town where emigrant wagons were fitted out. There was not a railroad within a hundred miles. By 1869, Omaha was the starting place for the transcontinental railroad journey.

"The railroad stretches west straight as an arrow from Omaha for five hundred miles, then for another 1,300 miles to the West Coast," Samuel Bowles wrote in his notebook. At the end of this trip he planned to write a travel book.

The train followed the Platte River Valley across Nebraska just as the wagon trains had. Hardly a tree could be seen from the train window, and the passengers remembered stories from the emigrants about having to find buffalo dung to build their cooking fires. Within a few years a Nebraska governor would proclaim a state holiday—called Arbor Day—just to plant some trees in this barren area.

Every twelve or fifteen miles the train passed a small building where there was a woodpile and a waterspout for the steam engine. About every hundred miles was a home depot that included an eating house, a few stores, and scattered houses. Villages that were large enough to be called cities were five hundred miles apart.

"Gathered around the depots," said Bowles, "are the invariable half a dozen, seedy staring loafers that are a sort of fungi indigenous to American railways."

Train-watching was only beginning to be a favorite occupation, but any sign of laziness had to be discouraged. Each time the train stopped at a station, a half dozen soldiers lined up, giving the passengers a secure feeling that they were protected from Indians. They had been told that only the Apaches of Arizona were still dangerous.

"There is more danger from masked gunmen," Bowles said. "But if any of them ever tried to rob a train, punishment would be so swift that no thieving band would try it again."

The train made a supper stop at Grand Island, but there was never time to order a meal, let alone sit down and eat. Most passengers ate from their own baskets of goodies and used the short stop for exercise, walking up and down the platform.

"Only two years ago this was a village of tents," Bowles said, as the train pulled into Cheyenne, Wyoming, only twenty-four hours after leaving Omaha. Now Cheyenne had small frame houses and a daily newspaper. The railroads had created the city for its main repair and supply shop. Its nearness to the mountainous part of the railroad was important, because winter would bring many unexpected and novel problems.

From Cheyenne to Ogden, Utah, the emigrant rode through wild, unknown territory. The engine chugged up the Black Hills to a pass that was the highest point the engine would have to climb, yet the country was open plains, and the engine seemed hardly to be struggling. Coming down into the plains around Laramie, the train stopped at a division station.

"I believe there will be a town here someday," Bowles spoke to a man near him. "Sportsmen, fishermen, and even invalids will flock to this climate."

Beyond the North Platte River, the scenery became high rolling desert country pocked with sagebrush. This was part of the trail that wagon train passengers had dreaded. The alkali turned their faces as brown as Indians and parched their lips. They had to beat and drag their cattle and horses to keep them from drinking the poisoned water. Crossing this 150-mile stretch by railroad in about eight hours, the train passengers felt none of the wagon emigrants' pain. Occasionally they still saw wagon trains—not everyone could afford to travel by the new railroad. Nothing made the train travelers feel better about the money they had spent for their tickets than to see the wagons moving at four miles an hour toward the destination that the train would reach in a few hours' time.

Everyone cheered as the railroad crossed the Continental Divide. From that point, all water flowed toward the Pacific Ocean. They watched the odd-shaped buttes and mountains in the distance all day, as the train tried to make up for time lost when the track curved and climbed. One of the landmarks along the wagon trail was Church Butte. The windswept rocks which resembled cathedrals looked very close, but actually

The railroad was completed at 3:05 P.M. (New York time) on May 10, 1869, with thousands of people watching

they were ten miles away. When the engineer stopped for the passengers to have a look, they quickly retreated back to the train. The wind was blowing hard and the sand blasted them with stinging force. At last the train came down out of the Wasatch Mountains and went along Weber Creek.

"Thousand mile tree!" sang out the conductor, and the train slowed. There was nothing for the passengers to see except a cedar tree with a sign on it, but it marked the halfway point from Omaha. Now only a little more than two days separated them from the Pacific Coast. The train moved on into the Salt Lake Valley and stopped at Ogden.

The most interesting sight in this valley was not the great desert or the salt lake, but the people. For several years, easterners had been suspicious of Mormons for their different ways, just as they were wary of all new religious beliefs. But in this valley the passengers could not help admiring the beautiful farms that flowered in the midst of desert dust and salt water.

Skirting the Great Salt Lake, the railroad climbed into the Promontory Mountains where, at Promontory Point, the Union Pacific and Central Pacific railroads had met only a short while before. The engine slowed down so everyone could see where the Golden Spike had been driven on May 10, 1869. The rest of the trip west would be over the part of the railroad that had been hardest to build.

Inside the cars, the passengers visited with each other and some tried to read, but it was hard to concentrate when someone was always shouting, "Look, an Indian . . . a teepee . . . there's a corral . . . and see the mining town." An occasional pigtail attracted attention and reminded the tourists of the part that Chinese workers had played in completing this difficult section of the railroad.

The train entered the East Humboldt Mountain valley at the

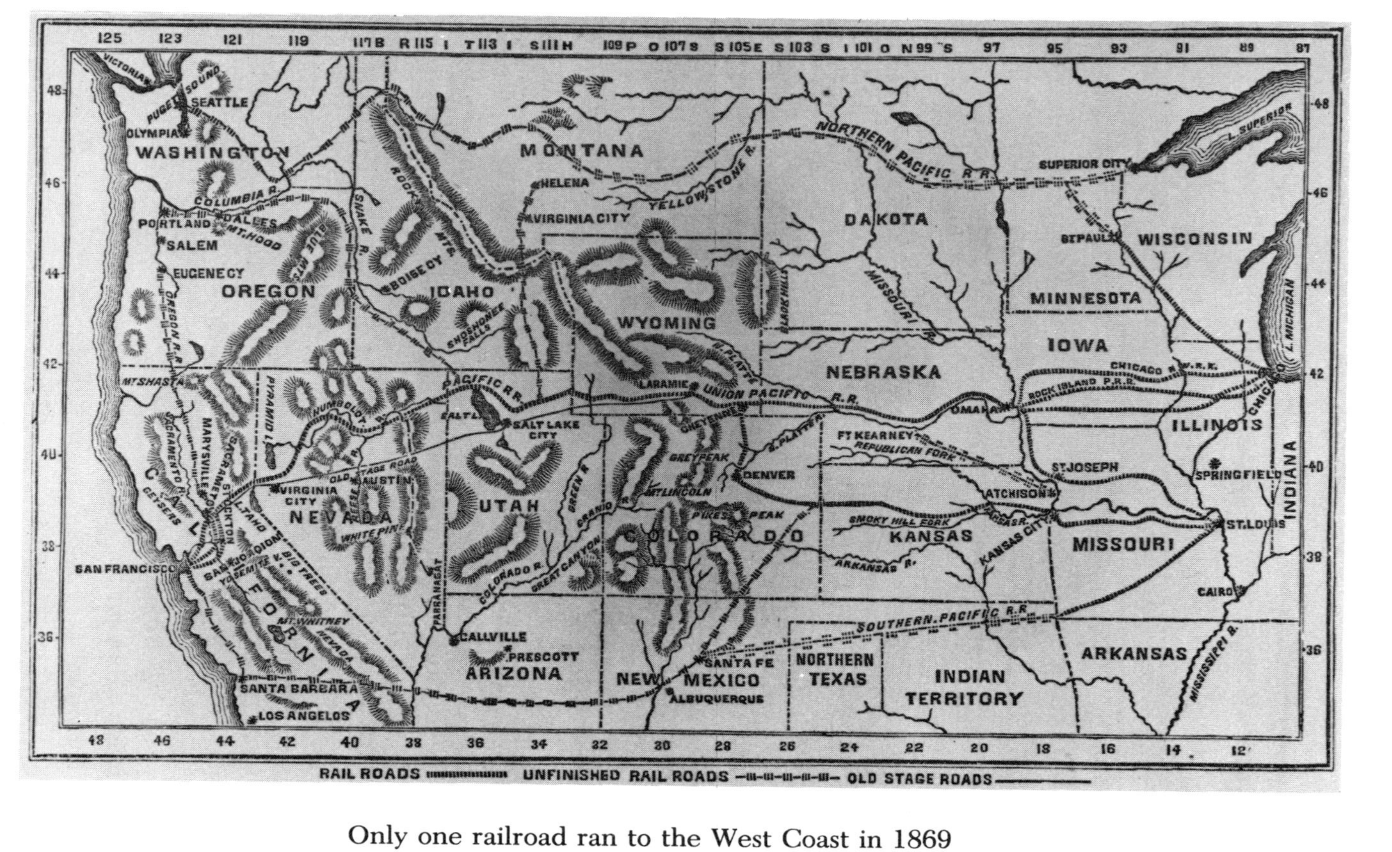

Only one railroad ran to the West Coast in 1869

When the engine burned up all the wood in a Sierra snowstorm, the passengers tore apart fences and found logs to fire it up again

town of Wells, where emigrant wagon trains still stopped for their first fresh water after crossing the desert. The railroad turned west and headed across another plain of sage brush and alkali flats toward the foot of the Sierra Nevada Mountains. The dry desert air made even the train passengers thirsty, and the engineer stopped for five minutes so everyone could have a drink from the Truckee River before the upward climb.

The engine crossed the Sierras near Donner Lake, where

several emigrants had died because of the disastrous snowdrifts. For about thirty miles along the highest part of the pass, the tracks had been roofed over for protection from deep drifts.

"It shuts out the best views," many passengers complained, but those who had traveled in the mountains in winter knew how important the sheds were. Two hundred miles of the most beautiful scenery imaginable now kept the passengers glued to their windows. The settlements they passed had slightly familiar names—less than twenty years before, the Gold Rush had taken place right along the creeks the train was crossing.

"I worked on this section of the track," one tourist told Samuel Bowles. "This piece along here cost a million dollars in gold—just for the blasting powder! In some places just one mile of track cost $300,000 to build."

Sometimes the builders had been forced to travel five hundred miles just to find timber for the ties. The nearest drinking water was often one or two hundred miles from the thirsty workers. Often there was no grass to feed the animals that helped them, and the iron for half the railroad had been shipped from the East around Cape Horn or across Panama.

At last the train came down into the Sacramento Valley. For the first time since leaving the East the passengers saw types of homes that looked familiar, white fences, flowering shrubs, trees, and nearby church steeples.

Samuel Bowles and the other tourists quickly found that life on the West Coast was not exactly as it was in the East. There were new phrases to learn, like "shebang" (for a shop, house, or office), "pans out" (succeeds), and "square" (perfect). The railroad track bound together the country as no other form of travel ever could.

3
Steamboating on the Ocean

The sea, the sea, the boundless sea,
So open, clear, and breezy!
(Whatever can this feeling be
which makes me so uneasy?)
—Source unknown

The First Ocean Steamers

John Stevens watched his *Phoenix* fondly as the steam poured from the stack amidships. This was the best boat he had built yet. It was obviously better than Fulton's *Clermont,* Stevens thought. Little wonder that Fulton had been giving him so much trouble.

The *Phoenix,* launched in April 1808, had been near enough to completion for steaming to Perth Amboy, New Jersey, in late September that year, but Stevens had built it to sail up and down the Hudson River. As long as Robert Fulton had a monopoly on the Hudson, there would be no future for the *Phoenix* there. Stevens put it away until the following spring, but the situation with Fulton was no better in 1809.

He gazed down at his ship from the hill where he lived in Hoboken, New Jersey. His son, Robert Livingston Stevens, managed it very well. Robert, now twenty-two years old, and his younger brother John had been sailing steamboats since their father had built them a tiny one called the *Juliana* in 1804. Stevens had hired Captain Moses Rogers for the *Phoenix,* but Robert had persuaded his father to allow him to be the

John Stevens' *Phoenix* became by chance the first American oceangoing steamboat

Phoenix's captain on the maiden voyage.

"But where can he sail her?" asked Stevens' friends. "Fulton has sewed up the entire river, and you'll never have a chance to try her out just in this harbor."

Stevens shook his head sadly. Even though the action had been somewhat illegal, the courts had upheld Fulton's petition for the right to have only his own steamboats on the Hudson. How could this tremendous river be "given" to any one man? There was plenty of space for competition there, but Fulton had wealthy and powerful friends. The monopoly could not last long, because the city of New York and its harbor would soon begin to grow. In the years ahead it might even be as important as Philadelphia.

"Philadelphia," Stevens answered. "That's where we'll take her."

On Saturday, June 10, the *Phoenix* left Hoboken, never to return. Robert had persuaded his father to let him captain it and he cast an anxious eye on the weather as the crew pushed off from the wharf. Soon the steam was up and the *Phoenix* moved gracefully to the quarantine ground off Staten Island and dropped anchor until noon on Monday. If Captain Moses Rogers was aboard at that time, none of the Stevens' family papers mention the fact. The only argument Robert lost to his father was over the elder man's insistence that a small schooner go along as an escort. Stevens had ordered its captain to save the crew of the *Phoenix* in case the small steamer turned out to be unseaworthy.

On Monday the wind was heavy and the waters choppy. After two hours of steaming, one of the starboard paddle wheels was damaged, so Robert turned into the quieter waters in the lee of Sandy Hook, anchoring in Spermaceti Cove while the crew repaired the buckets. The small schooner anchored nearby. By midnight the wheel was working and the heavy wind had calmed. Robert was anxious to get moving, and steamed over to talk to the captain of the schooner.

"We can't leave now," said the schooner captain. "There's no wind."

A grin spread across Robert's face. This was the chance he had been waiting for to prove that steamboats could move when sailboats could not. He ordered his crew to move off from the schooner. A few hours later the *Phoenix* passed the lighthouse at Sandy Hook and moved slowly into the ocean alone. Robert steered south along the New Jersey coast, moving about four miles an hour.

For twelve hours the little steamboat bucked the waves with the wind at its stern. The waves were showing white tops at four in the afternoon when Robert started across the bar at Cranberry Inlet. Just then the paddle wheel on the port side gave way and the relieved crew dropped anchor for the night.

There was still no sign of the schooner the next morning, and the wind was hard out of the south. Thursday, thunder and lightning crashed around the steamer and the rain poured down. Robert sent a small boat into the town of Tom's River for supplies. On Friday morning the schooner slipped into the inlet. Robert had the steam up, but the schooner's captain told him the ocean was rough outside. The wind kept shifting direction, and Robert knew that more stormy weather was brewing. By Saturday morning he could stand it no longer. At six the steamboat rode out from the inlet.

"Having no wheelhouse," reported a man who watched from the schooner, "she presented a very singular appearance, as the water—when she was in motion—would often be thrown as high as her smokestack."

Three hours of gale was enough. By nine Robert was glad to turn into the inlet of "Barny Gat" and drop anchor in the bay. It was Tuesday before the gale died down enough for the schooner to rejoin them. Before five on Wednesday morning, Robert had the *Phoenix* under way again, checking off gleefully the inlets they passed by. The wind died down, so the schooner never did catch up as they steamed on to Cape May and anchored for the night near the entrance to Delaware Bay. Thursday, Robert steamed up the Bay to New Castle, Delaware, but by Friday the boilers were fouled, and the boat floated ingloriously with the tide up to Philadelphia. The *Phoenix*'s ocean steamboating days were over, and it was fitted out with cabins to become a river steamboat.

"The steam coffin" was the name given by the seamen to the first steamer that was built to sail on the ocean. The *Savannah* was built in New York and launched on August 22, 1818. The same captain, Moses Rogers, who had once commanded the *Phoenix* had to travel all the way to New London, Connecticut, to find a crew willing to sail in the new steamer.

The *Savannah* was almost a hundred feet long and had three masts. In those days steam engines were used only when the wind failed. The paddle wheels were collapsible. They could be folded up and hauled onto the deck in about twenty minutes so they would not drag in the water when the sails were filled. The engine was used forty-one hours during the maiden voyage of eight and a half days from New York to Savannah, Georgia. But the steamer was unwanted. Its owners finally sold it to a firm in Liverpool, England.

The voyage to England took the steamer twenty-nine days and eleven hours. Unfortunately there was not a single passenger who had agreed to go on this speedy voyage. The ship's nickname had scared everyone away. The *Savannah* was steaming off the coast of Ireland, when a telegrapher took one look at the smoke and reported a ship on fire. A cutter went out to help, but could not catch up with the "burning" ship. When it arrived in England, Captain Rogers was surprised to see how many people wanted to look the ship over. Its fame had gone ahead—thanks to the telegrapher. But the buyers in Liverpool had had financial troubles and backed out of buying the ship. Once more it was unwanted. Captain Rogers sailed on to Norway, where a buyer supposedly waited, but once again the deal fell through. At last he sailed the ship back again —the trip took forty days—to Georgia. On this last trip he did not use the steam engine once, because coal and wood had been so expensive in Europe, until he entered the Savannah River. "The steam coffin" was just another invention that came on the scene before people knew they needed it. It was not a financial success, but it proved that steamboats could survive on the ocean.

Danger at Sea

The night of October 9, 1837, was no time to be at sea, even in a new steamer. The steamer packet *Home* was a floating palace with berths for 110 people. Just launched nine months before, the *Home* had already sailed twice to Charleston, South Carolina, in the record time of sixty-four hours. The *Home* left its New York dock at 5 P.M. on Saturday.

As the *Home* passed through the Narrows (where the Verrazano-Narrows Bridge is today) it struck briefly on a shoal, but was off again by ten. The captain ordered his men to make a thorough inspection to see whether there was any damage, but they found nothing wrong. All day Sunday the ship sailed south

"A huge wave broke over the stern like an avalanche," said one steamer passenger

down the coast without a problem. Then, as the *Home* approached Cape Hatteras, off the North Carolina coast, famous for its beaches that were lined with the bleached bones of ships, a gale was blowing.

The captain turned the ship more out to sea in order to round the Cape safely. Even though the ship had a very high forecastle, the waves began spraying the top decks, while the passengers huddled inside. Suddenly there was a cry from below.

"We're leaking!"

All hands that could be spared were ordered to start pumping. The male passengers volunteered to pump, but the leak only increased. Now the women began pumping. As soon as he thought they had passed Cape Hatteras, the captain ordered the ship turned toward shore in the hopes of beaching it. At the Cape, the islands slope slightly toward the west. Only a few miles farther along, and they might be protected more from the strong northeast wind that whipped the waves into a fury. The captain ordered all the sails set, but the ship was settling fast in the water. When the water reached the engines, only the sails would be left to move the ship toward the beach.

Passengers who were not bailing began cutting blankets into long strips to tie themselves to spars or anything else that might float. Four hours longer the ship labored toward the land, bending like a reed in the waves, until all the sailors thought each wave must surely break it in two. At ten that night the ship struck a shoal.

"In an instant," one passenger reported, "all was utter confusion and alarm. Men, women, and children screamed in a most agonizing manner. There were only three lifeboats and one of them had been smashed by the waves. Some people lashed themselves to spars on board and others made what struggle they could. One man threw off all his clothes but his shirt and pantaloons and swam ashore. Only two persons had life preservers and they were both saved."

The high forecastle was swept off the ship, and with it went about ten people, one of them the captain's wife. A heavy wave struck the floating section and five people fell off into the sea. One woman had tied herself onto the ship, and, when it broke up, the woman drowned because she could not untie herself. Ninety-five passengers died that night off the shores of Ocracoke Island.

Other ships and passengers were battling for survival off Cape Hatteras on that same night. An eyewitness on board the steam packet *Charleston* out of Philadelphia said that one huge wave broke over the stern of the ship like an avalanche.

"The bulkhead was broken in. Glass was shattered all over the ship. The water broke the skylights of the after cabin and poured through in torrents until the water was four feet deep. The deck of the wheelhouse was lifted fore and aft, leaving an opening an inch wide all around. Water poured through the slit with every wave and the ship rolled like a log in the water. The whole cabin was afloat with trunks, settees, and bonnet boxes washing from side to side."

"Start bailing quick," the captain hollered down. "Use anything—but bail fast."

It was vital to keep the water from rising enough to put out the fire in the steam boilers. Men and women stuffed mattresses and pillows into the broken portholes, but the waves only washed them out again. The captain came below for a minute, looking grim.

"We're going to run ashore," he shouted over the noise of the storm. "Everything depends on the character of the beach and your own self-possession and calmness to act with proper judgment at the trying moment. Meanwhile, keep bailing as long as you can. And don't give way to excitement. When you feel the ship strike ground, make for the bow *after* the next sea sweeps the decks."

The captain ordered the ship's carpenter to be ready with an ax to cut down the mast as soon as the ship struck. Then he returned to his place at the wheel.

"The boat rolled more than ever," a passenger recalled. "You could see it would not obey the helm. A constant stream of water swept the decks. The boat groaned and the bell rang with a sound peculiarly awful."

The passengers searched for ropes and fastened them around their bodies so they could tie themselves to anything that would float when "the trying moment" should come.

The captain found he could not get the ship toward shore because the wind was so strong from dead ahead. He ordered the engineer to raise more steam. All hope was gone if he failed. The passengers gathered up pieces of wood for the engine. So much had washed overboard that they had a hard time finding any. The sea had broken down doors and window frames, and these all went into the fire.

"With all the steam we could raise, we still could not steer for shore," one man said. "The wind and current carried us down along the shore, and this proved our saving."

At nine that evening the sea began to calm noticeably, and the ship reached quieter water. For two hours the captain headed as close to shore as possible. At last he ordered two anchors lowered until daylight came. Luckily the next morning was calmer. The *Charleston* made it into port.

Storms took their toll on sailing ships as well as steamers, particularly along the shores of Cape Hatteras. Although steamers had an advantage over sailing ships in a storm and against the wind, the captain of a sailboat could always say, "At least my ship won't explode!"

The steam packet *Pulaski* had left Savannah on June 13,

1838, headed north. The night was clear and so calm that the passengers had been enjoying a dance until eleven. Most had just gone below for a quiet night's sleep. Suddenly the peace was shattered by a tremendous explosion. The starboard boiler had blown up, taking with it that side of the ship and blocking the companionway. Boiling steam poured into the cabins, burning and killing several passengers.

A newspaper reported later that the ship had only four lifeboats. One was blown apart. Two left the scene with only a few people in them. The fourth was the only boat available for the rest of the survivors. Seventy-seven passengers died that night.

Charles Couper tells what happened to two of the *Pulaski*'s lifeboats that night. He had been visiting friends in Savannah and learned that Mrs. Frazer and Mrs. Nightingale were traveling with their children and maids northward on their annual trip to Newport, Rhode Island. They were to be on the same ship as he, and, being a gentleman, Couper told the ladies' husbands he would see the ladies safely to Rhode Island. The husbands were delighted for the escort, as southern ladies did not often travel alone. Most people who later heard Couper's story of how he saved the ladies and their children thought he had been courageous and completely in the right.

"We had just separated for the night," said Couper. "At the first sound of the explosion, I jumped up and ran on deck in shirt and trousers. Women were screaming. The deck was strewn with fragments. The vessel leaned badly to one side. I ran to the door of the ladies' cabin and called Mrs. Frazer. The ladies were only half-dressed, so I told them to dress quickly and be ready to follow and obey me.

"I quickly found two sailors and a boat, then hurried back to get the ladies, their children, and their maids. I told Mrs. Frazer to jump in the boat and threw her little boy in after her. Then I ordered Mrs. Nightingale to throw herself in the boat.

I jumped with Mrs. Nightingale's baby in my arms. We fell into the water, but managed to climb into the boat.

"I ordered the men to set the boat adrift . . . in spite of the shrieks and cries and commands and entreaties of the frantic crowds who were all endeavoring to get into it. The men obeyed me and began rowing while I steered. Soon we were astern of the ship. Another boat, filled with people, was near us. We watched the *Pulaski* sink.

"By daylight, we could see the breakers off the shore. We rowed toward shore all day. By afternoon the men at the oars were exhausted. Everyone wanted to get ashore, but I said not yet.

"We watched the other boat try. It capsized in the breakers, although we saw some of them make it to the beach. Rowing farther along the shore, I promised we would try to go in before sunset. There were breakers as far as we could see. Finally I made the men lie down and sleep before we made the final attempt.

"I tied Mrs. Nightingale's baby to her body, wrapping it round and round with a shawl. I charged one of the sailors with the care of Mrs. Frazer and her little boy. Then, with the sailors rested, we made the attempt to land.

"The boat capsized. Mrs. Nightingale sank. Twice I dived after her and caught her hair. When we reached the sand, I unwound Mrs. Nightingale's shawl and found her baby laughing on her bosom. Mrs. Frazer and her little boy were helped to shore by the sailor. She had grasped her little boy's wrist so tight that he bore marks on it for weeks after. We burrowed into the sand for warmth and lay there all night. The next morning we found help."

Charles Dickens' Luxurious Stateroom

When Dickens decided that he and his wife should visit the United States in 1842, and perhaps write a book about their trip, he went to a travel agent's countinghouse in London.

"You'll want the fastest ship—the mail steamer," said the agent, proudly showing Dickens a sketch of the American steam packet *Britannia,* bound for Halifax and Boston.

After studying the sketch, Dickens selected a roomy cabin, far from the potentially dangerous steam boilers, and put his money down on it.

On January 3, the Dickenses arrived at the dock with friends. They planned to put their baggage on board and then return to shore for a final good dinner at a restaurant. After a quick survey of the deck, they went below.

"This must be the breakfast room," said Dickens' friend as they reached the foot of the companionway.

"No, sir," said a steward. "This is the main saloon."

Dickens looked again at the narrow room. The ship's agent had shown him a picture with several ladies and gentlemen standing around in amiable groups. But this room looked more like a gigantic hearse with windows in the sides. At one end was a stove. Along the whole length was a long, long table with racks overhead stuck full of drinking glasses. Just the way those racks held on to the glassware so tightly hinted of the rolling seas that would make the trip dismal. But worse discoveries were to come.

The box they were shown to next was not anything like the attractive stateroom Dickens had selected at the agent's office. It had two berths, one above the other.

"Nothing smaller was ever made for sleeping—except a coffin," Dickens said. "The beds were covered with a very flat quilt. A very thin horsehair mattress was spread like a surgical plaster on the shelf."

Not only was there no sofa, and no place to store the two huge trunks, but not even one trunk fit in the room.

"By very nearly closing the door and twining in and out like serpents, and by counting the little washing-slab as standing room, we could manage to get four people into it all at one time."

At least the stateroom opened into the ladies' cabin, which was pleasant. A cheery fire warmed it, although it was dark. One of Dickens' friends said it was probably lighter at sea, but later Dickens said he could not for the life of him see why it should be. They watched, fascinated, as a stewardess pulled sheets and tablecloths from the insides of sofas and hidden lockers. Every piece of furniture was something else besides what it was intended to be, thought Dickens.

"I remember last January," the stewardess was chattering along without stopping. "No one was ever ill. Everybody danced from morning till night. It was a run of only twelve days—each one of them perfect."

Back on the icy shore once more, the Dickenses and their friends hurried on to their dinner. No one mentioned the weather or the trip ahead. Quietly though, Dickens decided to order something to eat that was "least likely to be converted into foreign and disconcerting material" when he was at sea the next day.

At 1 P.M. the next day the Dickenses took a small steamer out to the *Brittania,* which was by then anchored in the river. The ship was filled with passengers and their visitors, who had come to say good-by and to carry their last messages back on shore. Dickens loved meeting people, but he was not good in crowds.

"The packet was overrun with passengers swarming below

with their own baggage and stumbling over other people's; disposing themselves in wrong cabins and creating the most horrible confusion by having to turn out again; madly bent upon opening locked doors and on forcing a passage into all kinds of out-of-the-way places where there is no thoroughfare."

One old gentleman announced this was his fourteenth trip across the ocean, and many of the passengers regarded him as being quite an expert. Every time he looked up at the masts, they looked up too. When he looked over the sides, they did too, wondering whether he saw anything wrong.

"And," Dickens added, "hoping that in case he should, he would have the goodness to mention it."

As soon as the small steamer brought the captain from shore, a bell rang. Visitors were told to leave immediately and at least two thirds of the deck crowd climbed aboard the small boat to return to shore. They cheered the *Britannia* three times. The passengers returned the cheers.

"It would have been nice to leave on that high note," said Dickens, "but we had to wait another two hours before the mailbags were put on board."

At long last the captain appeared on the paddle box with his speaking trumpet. The officers all took their stations and even the cooks looked out to watch the moment of departure. Three more cheers came from the passengers.

"As the first one rings upon our ears, the vessel throbs like a strong giant that has just received the breath of life. The two great wheels turn fiercely round for the first time, and the noble ship, with wind and tide astern, breaks proudly through the lashed and foaming water."

All eighty-six passengers crowded into the main saloon to eat a hearty first meal, and at eleven most of them turned in, convinced they were pretty good sailors. The smells below were what Dickens called "an extraordinary compound." He would have stayed on deck the whole voyage if he could have, but finally he too went below. The ship had left the protected river and was now in the ocean.

"Two passengers' wives (one of them my own) lay already in silent agonies on the sofa. One lady's maid (my lady's) was a mere bundle on the floor. . . . Everything sloped the wrong way. I had left the door open a moment before . . . and when I went to shut it, it was uphill. Now every plank and timber creaked as if the ship were made of wicker-work."

For the next two days, Dickens did a lot of reading in bed, drinking cold brandy and water and eating hard biscuits. The third morning he was awakened by his wife shrieking.

"I look out of bed," he moaned. "The water jug is plunging and leaping like a lively dolphin. All the smaller articles are afloat except my shoes which are stranded on a carpetbag high and dry. Suddenly I see them spring into the air, and behold the looking-glass, which is nailed to the wall, sticking fast to the ceiling. At the same time the door entirely disappears and a new one is opened in the floor. The stateroom is standing on its head. Suddenly the ship rights. Before one can say 'Thank Heaven,' she wrongs again. And so she goes on staggering, heaving, wrestling, leaping, diving, jumping, pitching, throbbing, rolling, and rocking; and going through all these movements, sometimes by turns, and sometimes all together, until one feels disposed to roar for mercy. I call for the steward."

"What *is* the matter? What do you call this?" Dickens demanded of the steward when he arrived.

"Rather a heavy sea on, sir," said the steward, "and a head wind."

After the steward left, Dickens lay quietly, listening to the various domestic noises of the ship . . . "the breaking of glass and crockery, the tumbling down of stewards, the gambols overhead of loose casks, and the very remarkable sounds raised in their various staterooms by the seventy passengers who were too ill to get up for breakfast."

Just once Dickens found himself on the deck, trying to discover where the ocean ended and the sky began. He wasn't sure how he had gotten there. The captain came along and motioned to two burly seamen to get him below fast. The ship's doctor came and put a large mustard plaster on his stomach.

"The ship is flung on one side, springs up, rolls over on the other side, until a heavy sea strikes her with the noise of a hundred great guns, and hurls her back. She stops, staggers, shivers. Every plank has its groan, every nail its shriek, and every drop of water in the great ocean its howling voice."

About midnight one night Dickens, his wife, and a little Scottish lady were sitting in the ladies' parlor when suddenly a wave forced its way through the skylight. The hatch above burst open and the ocean came raging and roaring into the cabin. The little Scottish lady ordered the steward to tell the captain he must immediately have a steel rod attached to the top of every mast so the ship would not be struck by lightning. Soon the ladies were too sick to move. Dickens went to get some hot water and brandy for them.

"It being impossible to stand or sit without holding on, they were all heaped together in one corner of a long sofa. . . . They clung to each other in momentary expectation of being drowned. I approached with the glass. Suddenly they all rolled slowly down to the other end of the sofa. I staggered to that end, held out the glass, and suddenly they all rolled back again. I dodged them up and down the sofa fifteen minutes without once catching them, and by the time I did catch them, only a teaspoonful was left of the brandy and water."

When Dickens struggled up on deck the next morning everything was gray.

"A lifeboat had been crushed by one blow of the sea like a walnut shell and now hung dangling in the air. The planking of the paddle boxes had been torn sheer away. The wheels were exposed and bare and they whirled and dashed their spray about the decks at random. The bright-red chimney was white and crusted with salt. The topmasts were struck and stormsails set, the rigging all knotted, tangled, wet, and drooping."

Every day six or seven passengers gathered in the ladies' cabin to read, talk, or sleep. A ring of the bell at 1 P.M. announced the stewardess, who brought baked potatoes, roast apples, cold ham, salt beef, and hot collops. Another meal was at 5 P.M. Sometimes the passengers felt well enough to play whist, but since the cards would not stay on the table, the passengers had to put their tricks into their pockets. All the cabins leaked, and several berths were full of water.

On the morning of the sixteenth day, the ship steamed into Halifax harbor. For seven hours all was peaceful, then began the run "up" to Boston. Traveling the other direction—sailors called it going "down East," because the wind was usually behind—made the trip smooth and fast. Going toward Boston was rough and tumble. Dickens promised himself, when he set foot on the wharf at Boston, that he and his wife would go home in a sailing ship.

Steaming for Gold

Louis McLane hated to leave his beautiful Sophie behind, but he was going to San Francisco. In 1850 that was no place for a lady. He left with four hundred other gold seekers from New York on the steamer *Empire City* the seventeenth of February. Most of the passengers were farmers, many from Ohio and Wisconsin, all expecting after one season to return

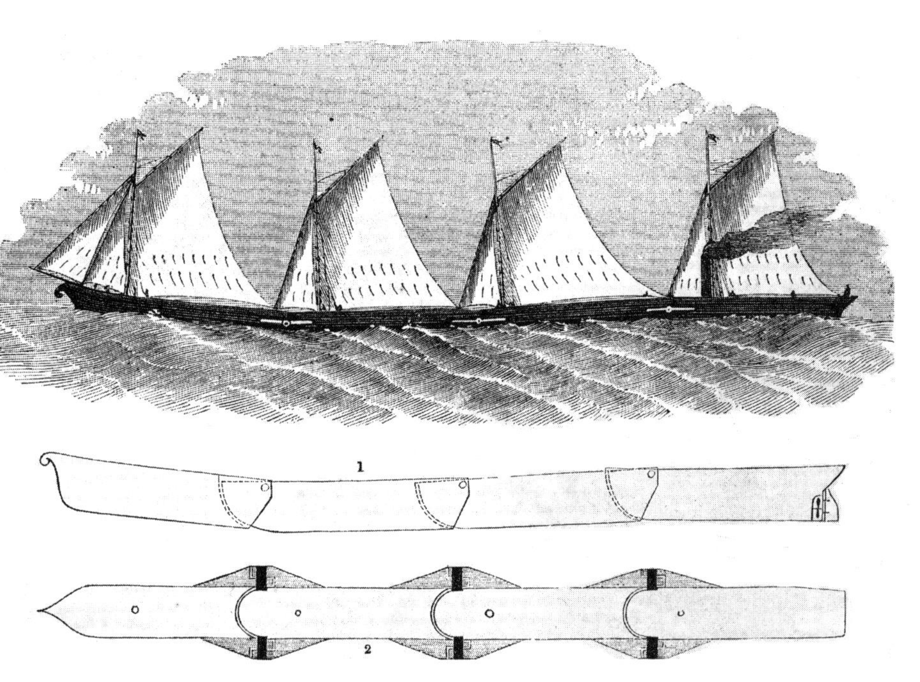

One suggestion for preventing seasickness was a "jointed steamship" that would ride the waves more comfortably
Fig. 1. Vertical section of the jointed steamship
Fig. 2. Horizontal section showing joint construction

east with pockets full of gold.

McLane was one of the few not planning to dig for gold. He was going to start his own steamboat company. He would collect gold in payment for taking miners up and down the Sacramento River to the goldfields. A few of the passengers had already been to the gold country, returned home, and were now on their way back again. McLane eagerly told them about the small steamboat he had brought aboard in pieces to be set up in San Francisco. They agreed that he would get rich carrying miners to and from their holdings in the valley.

"The waiter is just now ringing a large handbell," Louis wrote to Sophie, "and crying out at the top of his voice 'All gentlemen are requested to attend prayers on the quarter deck.' "

Louis followed the others, but his mind was more on the steam propeller he wanted to add to his boat than on the hymns. The captain was leading the prayers now. The way Louis saw it, he would find out first what sort of boat he needed and maybe return to the States to build it. He could carry it out in pieces, just as he was doing now with the *Erastus Corning*,

The New York newspapers were delivered to the departing steamer while under full headway

which he affectionately called the *E.C.* The worshipers were following some sort of ritual now which Louis had never seen in his church at home. The minister was one of the passengers, and Louis wondered vaguely what denomination he belonged to. The stewardess on this ship was just the kind of person he needed in his company. She was too old to marry and had a good temper. She had volunteered to stay with the men as a cook and housekeeper. At last the service ended, and Louis went back to finishing his letter to Sophie.

There was no place to "mail" a letter from a ship at sea, but if the ship put into a port, he could send it from there. Often two ships, going in opposite directions passed closely enough to "speak" one another. When that happened, the captains often exchanged newspapers and letters. At any rate Louis must have a long letter ready to go in a hurry in case he was lucky.

There were two ways to get to California by sea. One was to sail around Cape Horn, the tip of South America, in a sailing ship, a miserable voyage that took four or five months. In 1850, the fastest way was by steamship to Panama, about nine days, then across the Isthmus of Panama by walking or by boat (after 1855 there was a railroad) to the harbor on the Pacific. From there a steamer carried passengers to San Francisco and the "Gold Apple Field" in about thirteen more days. This was McLane's route.

Crossing the Isthmus of Panama was not quite so bad as McLane and the other men of his company had expected. What did surprise him was how differently Americans behaved when they were away from home. Friends whom he had thought very cultured suddenly developed such a rough exterior that he hardly recognized them. One young man from New York had been accused of stealing, and so was thrown into jail in Panama City. The accusation may have been true or false. At any rate, the person who accused him had left for the goldfields rather than wait around for the hearing a month away. So several of the young man's friends broke into the jail and hurried him onto the next ship. Most of the men felt that "Judge Lynch" was the best way.

"Such affairs as these give Americans a bad name," McLane told his wife.

Most men were so anxious to get to California that they paid almost any price for a ticket. One man sold his $125 ticket for $300. The buyer sold it for $400, and that third man who bought it refused to sell it for even $600. McLane had been able to get a ticket only on the *Sarah Sands,* a slow sailer out of Panama. Now he was able to sell that ticket and buy "deck passage" for $300 on the steamer *California.* A deck passenger had the privileges of the cabin, such as eating, but had to sleep anyplace he could find. McLane found a friend with a large stateroom on board and put up a folding cot. The *E. C.* had to follow on a slower ship.

The *California* left on March 2 for San Francisco—McLane spelled it "St. Francisco." The sea was calm and he was excited about the way the steamer behaved in this pacific ocean. This was the ocean where he would run his own steamers soon.

"This is certainly the ocean for steam," he told his wife. "Light airs and smooth water. But the heat is the death of the firemen. The air in the engine room is 104° to 122°, depending on the breeze. It is 130° in the fireroom. The poor firemen come up on deck at the end of their watch looking utterly exhausted, and throw themselves, dripping with perspiration, under a windsail and lay there until they cool."

On March 10, the *California* stopped at Acapulco, Mexico, for coal. The steamer had been moving along at almost eight knots. No man could have made the trip across the country by land nearly so fast as by steamboat, thought McLane.

When the *California* stopped at Cabo San Lucas, at the southern end of Lower California, the passengers saw some very unhappy travelers aboard the steamer *Chesapeake.* This ship had left Panama a month before the *California*, but had run out of fuel. Finally it had limped into this port and now had barely enough fuel to get to San Diego. Its passengers begged those on the *California* to sell their tickets and offered ridiculous prices, but no one took them up on their offers. (Those passengers finally sued the company for sending such a hulk out to sea and for losing them money they might have made

Crossing the Isthmus of Panama was not so bad as Louis McLane had expected. Soon steamers made it even swifter

digging in the goldfields. It was June before any of them reached San Francisco.)

On Saturday, March 30, the passengers on the *California* awoke to discover thick fog. Fog meant one thing—land must be near. By ten in the morning the fog cleared enough for the ship to run through the Gate, which later would be renamed the Golden Gate.

"There were three hundred fifty ships at anchor," McLane told his wife. "When I was here before in 1847, the town had about a hundred houses. Now there are 20,000 people and a 'floating population' living on the ships of 15,000 more. I did not recognize one single spot on the shore."

But it was steamboats that interested McLane most. He saw some that he would not have boarded back East plying up and down the rivers and bay. They charged such enormous fares that he figured even a small steamboat could pay for itself in less than two months. One called the *Mint* was only fifty feet long, but had been sold for $10,000. Two weeks later it was sold for four times that amount. The *Mint* earned its owners $1,000 a day!

McLane could hardly wait to get started with his own steamboat company, but the other members of his enterprise were on the slow boat, the *Sarah Sands.* His house, in pieces, was on board the *Hampden,* and his steamboat, in pieces, was on the ship *Green Point.* They all arrived months after he did. By the end of June, the house and office were built, and the *E.C.* was floating by September.

"I bought an old Spanish bell from a mission," he told Sophie. "One of those with a deep, soft tone so rarely to be heard outside of Spain. She will be known by her bell before she comes in sight of a landing."

4
Touring by Trolley

Riding one morning my fare I'd just paid,
Gave up my seat to a sweet little maid,
Tho' she was really a stranger to me
Soon in a deep conversation were we.
—Elsie from Chelsea
Harry Dacre, 1904

From Horses to Electric Trolleys

The earliest horsecars were mostly ugly wooden boxes with wooden benches running down each side for passengers. Only a few horsecar companies tried to make their carriages glamorous.

The New York and Harlem Railroad Company began its street railway in 1831. Within a year, passengers crowded into its attractive cars, each marked on the outside with the company president's name, John Mason. Passengers admired the padded seats and large glass windows. Many of them did not have as comfortable seats at home. But, even though several distinguished citizens rode in the cars, no one thought the street railway was the start of an important idea.

In 1853, New York City held the first world's fair in the United States—the Crystal Palace exhibition. The horsecars carried thousands of fair visitors up Fourth and Sixth avenues to the Crystal Palace, which was well north of the city, at Fifth Avenue and 42nd Street. After the fair, many horsecar riders returned home and asked for a horsecar railway in their own cities. For the next forty years horsecars were the best way to

DOWN TOWN R.R.
ROUND TOWN
UP TOWN

The "bob-tail" car looks harmless,
but don't argue with the driver

Don't try to ride with the box
and bundle fiend

Bob-tail, like time, waits for no man

Walk your horse on curves and switches

Drivers are not fond of changing bills

move people from place to place in large cities.

"Bob-tail" cars were only about ten feet long and had no rear platform. They were pulled by one horse, and the overworked driver had to take the fares and make change. On the larger trolley cars, the driver stood on an open platform in rain and snow, holding the hand brakes with one hand and the reins with the other. A wood-burning stove on the back platform sent heat through registers into the car. Passengers entered through the rear door and paid their fare to the conductor.

Horsecars left behind a trail of manure that added to the street dust on dry, windy days. Doctors said that the manure caused many illnesses. The driver's constant clanging of the bell, meant to warn pedestrians out of the way, was blamed for giving people nervous diseases. When the weather was too hot, the horses often collapsed in the street, blocking traffic and causing a crowd of angry people to gather. Such incidents resulted in the horsecar companies being fined for mistreating their animals, and they ordered their drivers to walk the horses very slowly on hot days. Traffic also slowed down because farmers fitted their wagons exactly into the "bob-tail" car tracks and refused to move out of the way.

Strange sounds frightened horses, and cities provided an endless supply of sudden noises, from factory steam vents to runaway carriages and shrieks from passengers. When startled, the horses drawing the "bob-tail" cars bolted and plunged wildly down the street, yanking a dangerously wobbling car behind. In many cities, where Sunday was ordained a quiet day, horsecars, with their endlessly ringing bells, had to stop altogether. Philadelphia citizens complained that the only day they had to ride the cars was Sunday, so the mayor agreed to allow horsecars after 1 P.M., but without any bells and with the horses walking slowly past every church.

Horses were also liable to sicknesses, like the "epizootic" that struck every horse in Boston one year. With the horses out of business, the firemen had to pull the fire engines by hand. The trolley car conductors volunteered once to pull the trolleys by hand but were glad to be turned down.

By the 1860s, it was perfectly respectable for a lady to ride, unescorted, in one of the city trolley cars. The ladies who could not afford carriages were so happy to have a means of travel

Baltimore's first horsecars were free, until passengers tried them and liked them

that they often took their shopping baskets and passed up their local grocery stores for the chance to shop somewhere new. Even wealthy ladies enjoyed the independence of using the trolley rather than having the driver hitch up the carriage and riding in grander style to pay a morning call on a friend.

Everyone loved the new electric trolleys. The almost silent cars brought an entirely different kind of life into—and out of —America's cities. Doctors announced there was much less sickness without so many horses around. In 1890, fifteen thousand horses pulled trolleys—just in New York City, although some cities had experimented with electric trolleys. By 1894, most trolley tracks began to extend out from cities into the country. The farmlands beyond the city limits were now upgraded to "suburbs."

Electric trolley cars usually had fourteen double seats, seven on each side of the aisle, like railroad cars. In the winter they were heated by electricity, and in summer the windows were taken out to let the fresh air blow through. Often the windows were not put back in until it snowed.

People loved trolleys because they were tired of the noise, smoke, and cinders of the steam railroads. Although trolleys were confined to a track like the railroads, they gave much more independence to their riders. A trolley conductor would let a passenger off anywhere along the road, even though it was not a regular stop. Some conductors even did errands for their customers—taking a country lady's shopping basket into the city to fill it with her list of needs from a dry goods store, or taking a city lady's basket out to the country to fill it with fresh strawberries or vegetables.

"I am paid to run the car, of course," said one conductor in 1901, "and to keep the schedule as well as I can. But where we do not have many crowds, and where the patronage is rather regular, we get to know the people as well as we do our own relatives. The conductor naturally takes pride in his own popularity. I have people who will not ride on any car but mine if they can help it, and while that does not seem to mean much in money, it does mean a good deal of satisfaction. When Christmas comes around, or the fruit season comes on, I can take home a nice basket to my wife and the little ones almost every night. I find that kindness pays."

The conductor's friendliness had much to do with making the trolley car so popular. People had fun on trolleys. They visited with the conductor and with each other. The same people would never have dreamed of talking and joking with each other on the railroad, where they remained strangers.

In many cities, like New York, trolley riders were not allowed to smoke. William Abbott became very angry one day when a man climbed aboard a trolley and stood on the back platform smoking a cigar.

The friendly conductor made the trolley cars instantly popular

"You can't smoke here," said Abbott.

"Why not? I'm outside," the man answered. Abbott turned to the conductor for help, but since it was a "pay as you enter" car, the conductor was more than busy collecting money and pounding his foot lever. The two men argued and soon the entire car joined in. When the man got off at 42nd Street, Abbott got off with him and called a policeman, demanding that the smoker be arrested.

"On what charge?" the man asked angrily.

"The section of the Penal Code that prohibits offending the occupants of a public stage or car," Abbot answered swiftly.

"I'm afraid I have to arrest you, sir," said the policeman. "This same gentleman made me arrest an inspector last week." The man spent two hours in jail and paid a two-dollar fine.

Trolley cars had a personal touch that railroads could never compete with. Mrs. Mary Stewart took a trolley ride one hot day in Pawtucket, Rhode Island, in 1901. Ice-cream cones had not been invented yet, but certainly this kind of day made a person think of ice cream.

"We passed by an ice-cream pedlar," says Mrs. Stewart. "The motorman slowed down. The conductor and most of the men in the car jumped off. The men brought back to each of the women some ice cream in a pasteboard carton with a tin spoon on top."

The heavy trolley cars with plows attached could clear the way for other traffic through even the heaviest snowfall, an asset that had its disadvantages when carts and carriages slowed them down.

Trolleys had one powerful enemy—the railroads. In places where the trolley tracks had to cross over the railroad tracks, the competition was often deadly. When railroad employees tore up the trolley tracks that had been laid down the day

After a snowstorm, the only clear path was the trolley tracks—carts and carriages created slow, single-file traffic before, the trolley company laid new tracks that night. Then tough gangs hired by both sides hid in the bushes waiting for the next move. Sheriffs in small towns everywhere busily hauled the fighters off to jail. Finally the matter was settled in court, and trolleys were given the right to cross railroad tracks where necessary.

The same sort of fights broke out between rival trolley lines. The Belleville (Illinois) Suburban Line ran parallel with the Day Line (from Belleville to St. Louis) along one piece of turnpike. When the Suburban Line claimed it owned the turnpike, the Day Line cut its fare from 20 cents to 5 cents and filled its cars with customers. The Belleville Suburban Line responded by carrying one hundred tough men out into the country, where they began tearing up the tracks of the Day Line. Naturally the Day Line sent out more than a hundred men to help hold down their tracks. When the men from Belleville Suburban saw the carloads of men approaching, they tried to pull the rails out from under the Day Line trolleys. But the current was turned on and they got several bad shocks. The incident ended with fractured skulls, and the sheriff arrived with a writ against the Suburban Line. Days in court and a few more in the hospital finally ended the competition between these two lines and other warring trolley lines across the country.

The other trolley car problems were more easily solved. Electricity was not to be trusted in the 1890s, whether it was on the street above the trolley car or in the home. Occasionally, especially on a rainy day, someone got a bad shock in a trolley car. This problem was solved by using better insulation. Once in a while the driver of an electric automobile got the idea of charging his car from the electric wires of the trolley line, but he would get such a bad shock that few drivers tried the same trick.

"Tie up your dogs or the trolley may turn them into sausage

meat," said a country newspaper when trolleys first ran out of the city. More people were concerned that trolleys would hit absentminded pedestrians. They demanded that trolleys install a net to swoop up people who stepped in front.

A Day of Fun

Trolley companies needed ideas to make the public give up horse carriages and take their new cars instead. Empty trolleys did not earn money.

At first people were happy just to ride out into the country. For the first time in their lives, city people who had never been able to afford a horse and carriage were able to look on the mansions of the rich who lived outside the crowded city. On Sundays, the only day men did not work, whole families of gaping city dwellers stared at the world outside their own narrow streets. Papa usually carried a hamper of food, and the children eagerly pointed out places where they could eat their picnic supper. The trolley's clanging gong added to the excitement. Coming home at twilight, with the trolley's electric lights turning night into day inside the car, was a thrill easily worth a dime.

Just as excited as the city people were the country people who had never been to the city. A large number of them now ate dinner at city hotels and restaurants, returning afterward to their country homes. Young men from the country could now work in the city and know that the trolley would run cheaply in all sorts of weather.

Builders and real estate agents boosted trolley rides to country areas where they wanted to sell building lots. On a Saturday afternoon, hundreds of people boarded the trolley for a free ride to a point outside the city. Clutching their food hampers, they left the trolleys to the sounds of a band hired by the builders to provide a party atmosphere. After lunch, topped off with free ice cream supplied for the express purpose of getting all the people together in one spot, the builders pointed out the many advantages of buying a lot in this pleasant development. As they spoke, they directed the audience's attention to the street curbs and signposts already installed. They waved vaguely toward where the school, churches, fire engine house, and other important buildings would be built. Many lots were sold at trolley picnics.

Trolley parties began in 1895. An individual or group rented a trolley car for ten dollars for the evening and sent out invitations. The best parties hired at least two cars—one for the band. The partygoers left from the terminal in the city, cheered on by a large crowd that had gathered just to watch the fun. The cornet band hired to follow the party almost drowned out the cheers and exploding firecrackers.

Sometimes partygoers dressed in masquerade costumes or in evening attire. They amused the residents whose homes they passed as well as themselves. A trolley party did not pass by very quietly. As many as eighty parties often traveled along the same twenty-mile route on a summer evening.

In the old days these same parties would have competed for the road by racing their horses and buggies to the party place. But there was no way to have a racing competition between trolleys running on the same track. So the competition came in the form of decorations. Each group wanted its party distinguished from the other parties along the same track. The price for a trolley party doubled quickly to $22.50 and up. For another ten dollars the trolley company provided the decorations—clover leaves for St. Patrick's Day, a horse motif for a trip to the horse show, bunting and flags for patriotic parties, and Chinese lanterns for a carnival look. The guests dressed up to match the theme.

An illuminated trolley, a clown, a band made an instant party

The evening's fun began with the ride out to the party place, often a hotel several miles from the city. There the trolley unloaded and retired to a siding. The guests had dinner and danced, often to the music of the band they had brought along. The ride back home was usually considerably louder than the ride out had been. Young people who would never have raised their voices in a drawing room felt quite anonymous in a trolley.

Daytime trolley parties carried hordes of people to baseball games, shooting matches, bicycle races, and the circus. A big event could easily fill twenty trolleys in a row. Even a Baptist Sunday school picnic to a park filled the trolleys with five thousand passengers.

Excursion tours attracted people who could not afford a carriage of their own. For 75 cents each the all-day excursion included a stop for a picnic dinner at a woodsy place and an hour's stop at a mineral spring hotel where there were boat rides, dancing, and a merry-go-round.

Trolley excursions became so popular that all across the country the companies planned new trips for their passengers. They often handed out booklets listing the many sights waiting for the family on a day's trip. A Boston family could go to Nahant for the day and have a famous fish dinner. No other ride could advertise that its trolley cars traveled within ten feet of Massachusetts Bay for two miles. An excursion up the Connecticut River valley climaxed with a trolley ride up to the summit of Mt. Tom, which, the trolley brochure claimed, was even better than the Alps. Still another excursion carried Bostoners to "Historic Plymouth—Land of the Pilgrims' Pride." The one dollar paid for the round-trip ticket included a stop at "Mayflower Grove" along the way, where passengers saw two performances daily at a rustic theater or a band concert on Sundays.

"Don't fail to visit Lincoln Park on the 'Gee Whiz Line,' " read one advertisement, promising the passengers dancing, open-air theater, and countless delights. The most historic trolley ride in New England was on the Paul Revere Short Line which followed Paul Revere's horseback route. This line had an observation trolley to Concord and Lexington and included a one-hour ride on a barge at Concord.

When trolley companies planned which direction to stretch their tracks out from cities, they bought up cheap land to build amusement parks. Almost every large city had at least one special park to ride to on the trolley. Washington, D.C., had its Glen Echo Park; Pittsburgh had Kennywood Park, and Boston had Norumbega.

The conductor and the motorman get set for the crowds that will go to Willow Grove Park to hear Sousa's band

"New Open-Air Theatre, largest and finest in the world," boasts a 1910 advertisement for Norumbega Park, where tourists also found "an elegant café, a mysterious chalet, and power boats and canoes for boating on the Charles River."

In the wealthy community of Chestnut Hill, just outside the Philadelphia city limits, one trolley company built an amusement area called "The White City." All the buildings, from the casino to the bandstand, were painted a stark and sanitary white. Its green grass was kept mowed by a herd of cows belonging to a neighboring farmer. Unfortunately the cows took a liking to the white paint which they licked constantly, and soon they died of lead poisoning. Meanwhile the wealthy community was so outraged to have the amusement park bringing crowds of city people to its neighborhood that residents banded together, bought up the trolley company, and tore down the park.

The trolley company that built Willow Grove Park in another area was very careful to avoid the same mistake. Willow Grove was noted for its refined atmosphere. Its customers were expected to dress up and mind their manners. Only the finest music was played in its music pavilion, because the park's founders believed that good music "roused the nobler passions" of their fellowman.

On the days that Victor Herbert or John Philip Sousa conducted their orchestras at the Park, over 30,000 people flocked

Willow Grove Park was not built for "fun," but to "rouse the nobler passions" of its patrons

there on the trolleys. The band shell, constructed of thousands of small wooden strips, amplified the music all over the park with a mellow tone that no electronic amplifier ever reproduced. When the orchestra played the national anthem or Sousa's "Stars and Stripes Forever," a large metal American flag on the front of the platform lighted up with hundreds of red, white, and blue electric bulbs. The sight thrilled the audience into patriotic fervor, one of the "nobler passions" the park intended to rouse.

To control any baser passions, the park kept its own contingent of fifty guards and had a small jail on the grounds. No liquor was sold or allowed in the park. On the hottest day of summer any man or boy who removed his coat and tie was taken to the nearest gate. One guard patrolled the aisles of the band shell and removed anyone caught snickering or talking loudly during concerts.

The Midway was filled with amusements. There was a trip through "Venice" in a gondola that floated along canals through flower gardens and past Venetian buildings. The "Mountain Scenic Railway" began as a roller coaster and ended with a trip through an underground tunnel with occasional glimpses into lighted passageways. One mother took her young son for a trip through "The Coal Mine," not knowing that the slow ride now terminated in a wild roller coaster ride. After a word to the manager about misrepresenting the ride, she retired quickly to the comfort station, where the attendant politely replaced all the hairpins that had fallen out of her hair.

Moving pictures were so new in 1909 that a favorite attraction at the park was called "Tours of the World." The "passengers" sat in what looked like the last two coaches of a railroad train and faced a screen where they saw moving pictures taken from the front of a moving train. The most popular amusement for people who did not have the newfangled automobiles of their own was "The Automobile Race." They rode on real autos, pulled by cables, along four parallel wooden tracks. The riders jeered and cheered as they passed each other moving up to twenty-five miles an hour.

A peaceful change from the Midway was the picnic grove and the two lakes where canoeists and rowboaters could show off their muscles. In the evening an electric fountain in one of the lakes was lit by colored lights, sending home the park patrons with enough of the "nobler passions" to last all week.

The Poor Man's Automobile

While wealthy men granted interviews with newspaper reporters to talk about their automobile trips over the worst roads in the world, the poor man was able to travel almost anywhere in the country by trolley car for mere pennies.

"Automobiling is a brave pastime for the rich who do not mind getting down on their backs in the road and hammering straight up at bolts and things, with grease dripping down their faces," said John Jones, a trolley car lover. "Wheeling is good sport, but there are punctures to contend with. The railroad is okay if you are willing to forgo pleasure and endure smoke and cinders. As for me, I'll take the trolley."

Jones had spent ten cents on a guidebook called the *Trolley Wayfinder*. It told him the distance from one town to the next, the fare, how long it would take him to get to each point along the line, and how to change from one trolley line to another.

Jones's trolley out of Boston toward Worcester, Massachusetts, was unusually comfortable. On each side of the aisle was a single row of wicker chairs with soft cushions. They were not attached to the floor like most railway car seats, but could be faced any direction and moved about for convenience. A glass door separated the riders from the motorman.

"When I was ready to stop for the night," Jones said, "I just asked the conductor which was the best hotel in town."

Traveling from Worcester to Hartford, Connecticut, he had to wait an hour in a town called Brookfield. As long as he was stuck there, he decided to roam into a nearby antique store. Three hours later he returned to the trolley line, his arms filled with treasures he could not resist. The trolley carried him to Springfield, Massachusetts, and down the Connecticut River to Hartford. His trip was broken only for about fifteen miles when he had to take a railroad into New Haven. From there to New York the trolley ride was unbroken—a twenty-two hour ride that cost about $7.50.

"Best take three days for the twenty-two hour ride," Jones advised his friends. "You can enjoy it more. Many old people are still afraid to ride on the railroad, but they love the trolleys. For one thing they know the driver will stop long enough for

This double-deck trolley car carried 110 people to the zoo in Pittsburgh

them to get on and off safely. He'll also stop if your hat blows out the window or if you forget something."

Jones had to force himself to go on to New York. At one point he could have turned off on a series of trolley car rides that would have led him through Niagara Falls to Ohio, Indiana, and Michigan.

Wise trolley travelers headed for good summer hotels and avoided the business hotels. They relaxed and laid out the next day's ride so they could reach a pleasing small town or summer resort by evening. Trolleys ran all the time and no reservations were necessary. A traveler could get off anyplace that appealed to him and continue at any hour. Although it was possible to travel 150 miles in a day, that was not so much fun as two or three shorter trips, with time off to explore a pretty road or have lunch at an attractive village.

"I love the country trolleys—not the city ones," said Sarah Preston in 1904. "The car jumps, jolts, bumps, and thumps. It swings and sways through meadows. I love to watch the passengers change. It's interesting to watch the different people —the vulgar mingle with the distinguished."

As she thumped along, she noted down all the changes outside her trolley window. She counted the rocking chairs on the porch of a summer hotel as the trolley clanged through an old village. Next year, she decided, she would take the trip she had been planning for so long—from New York to Boston.

"There is no train to catch, no dirt or smoke. Just God's free air and sunshine all day," Sarah reported after her first day on the trolley the next summer. She had begun at the railroad station in Connecticut, just to get outside New York City faster, although she could have taken the trolley the whole way from her apartment.

"We were flying through the woods almost at once."

At Bridgeport she got off for lunch and then boarded another trolley. Being a New York apartment dweller, Sarah was surprised at the number of single homes in Connecticut.

"There were little wooden cottages of eight rooms or less, with as much out-of-doors roofed over as each owner could pay for. These are the homes of tomorrow's homemakers," she thought as she watched the happy barefoot children and their mothers in "wash-gowns" sitting on their porches, sewing and visiting with each other. Grandparents got off the trolley to be greeted by laughing children. "Low-voiced gentlewomen" got on with their baskets of eggs to take to market. Ladies no longer wore sunbonnets or farmers high-cut overalls. Things were changing in the country, and the trolley was going to bring more changes.

"Automobile travel just isn't the same," Sarah said to a lady sitting next to her. "You lose the people when you climb into a motorcar and drive alone."

Just as with other inventions, someone always asked "Yes, but what are they good for?" Trolley companies were very quick to find out what trolleys could do well.

In several large cities, they were used to deliver the mail. A few young couples tried trolley weddings, but they were not very popular. Cities like Terre Haute, Indiana, tried double-deck trolleys. Milton S. Hershey ran trolley cars to carry his employees to and from work at his chocolate factory, and at other hours the trolleys delivered fresh milk to the plant. One of the most spectacular trolley trips in the world was a circular route to visit both sides of the Niagara Falls Gorge.

A few cities put parlor cars on trolley tracks, with upholstered wicker armchairs and the interior finished in rich mahogany. In Manchester, New Hampshire, a person could rent such a parlor car for a sightseeing party for five dollars a day. In Chicago two men offered a luxurious trolley car to rent for parties, which included a buffet car, a complete kitchen, and

In 1866, New Yorkers saw this tempting trolley that might carry them above Broadway to Central Park, but it remained on paper

a porter to pamper the sightseers.

Among the ideas that worked was the funeral trolley. Several cities used a somber black- or brown-painted car, with the motorman and conductor outfitted in black uniforms, to carry the coffin and mourners to the cemetery. The ordinary charge for carrying the coffin alone was $100, but for $15 to $40 the bereaved family could hire the funeral trolley and carry everyone. The coffin lay behind a heavy glass door, and there was a window overlooking the street for displaying the flowers. A large compartment held twenty-four mourners, and a smaller one, divided from it by heavy black drapes, held the family. The trolley waited on a spur at the cemetery and carried the mourners back home again.

Trolley car admirers thought a great future awaited trolleys. Soon tracks extended so far into the country that a person could almost cross the United States on trolley cars alone. But

John Jones had an idea for the future of trolleys that was a little more personal.

"Someday we will see the house trolley," he spoke confidently. "The car, made to look like a little home with several rooms, will make the ideal summer home. It will be guided here and there by the occupant who will carry his own set of rails. When he reaches a pleasant spot, he will lay down the rails to make a temporary spur. Then he can drop anchor in a lovely meadow, get out his fishing pole, and sit on the rear platform and fish."

Unfortunately trolley cars did not survive long enough for Jones's "house trolley." The trolley car was just beginning to take hold on the public in 1908, when Henry Ford invented an automobile that nearly everyone could afford. Eventually buses displaced trolleys from the rural routes.

5
The Merry Automobile

He was her slave this chauffeur brave
She was a touring maid;
Gloved hands in lap, in leather cap
And dust-proof gray arrayed.

"Twin cylinder," he said to her,
"My heart's a motor true,
Which drives unseen, Life's gasoline,
Through all my veins for you."
—*Motor* magazine, May, 1905

Never So Good as a Bicycle

The year 1899 was the end of a remarkable century. Travel had been made so comfortable and easy with steamboats, railroads, and ocean liners that few people could picture another invention coming along to improve on such modern marvels. The harebrained notion of a "horseless carriage" seemed least likely to be an improvement.

"The ordinary horseless carriage is at present a luxury for the very wealthy," it was noted in a letter that year. "Although its price will probably fall in the future, it will never, of course, come into as common use as the bicycle."

Many people were even suspicious of the bicycle. A minister in Indianapolis banned the bicycle for women in his congregation because, he said, the ladies had to wear shorter dresses "than the laws of morality and decency permitted." He had even seen the ankles of some women as they pedaled on the public street.

A police captain in Chicago said women were in danger of showing more than their ankles.

"Women of refinement," he said about lady bicyclists, "are

thrown among the uncultivated and degenerate of both sexes. Their coarse, boisterous and immoral gestures are heard and seen while they speed along our streets and boulevards."

Girls pleaded with their fathers to believe that signaling with their arms to cyclists behind them and waving to people they passed were not meant to be immoral gestures. They promised to wear thick striped stockings just in case their ankles might come uncovered while pedaling. But many girls could only hope that some other vehicle might come along to give them some of the freedom that boys enjoyed.

In New York City, the famous Fifth Avenue stageline added one hundred horseless electric cabs in February of 1899. The year before, the company had tried thirteen horseless cabs as an experiment, and everyone was surprised to see how popular they were. Doctors said they were a boon to public health, and getting rid of horses would mean less dust, mud, cobblestones, and noise on the city streets. There would be fewer nervous diseases, too, because the electric cabs ran on large pneumatic tires and were almost silent.

During the harsh winter storms they behaved very well, running all night long, even when the snow was ten inches deep. The electric cabs took many of the horse cab company's calls, because it was so dangerous for the horses to be out in the snow and ice. However, the cab company found that the electric cabs were always sitting in the terminal getting charged up. Twenty-five miles was as far as one could go on a single charge, and in winter they did not do that well.

At first everyone wanted electric cars. They were not likely to explode, like the steam car or the gasoline car. They traveled over the road "in a velvety sort of way," wives explained to their husbands, and they did not even need a strong arm to crank the engine.

There was no definite name yet for the new contraptions.

"Automobile fever" inspired several new books for young people, like *Automobile Girls at Newport*

Some people thought they ought to be named like yachts—the *Matilda* or *Hobo.* Their horses had always been called by their names, and it would be nice to have the horseless carriage with a nameplate on its back. Even the word "auto-mobile" had not been decided on. Other suggestions included Electromobile, Ipsomotor, Self-Motor, Auto-go, and Autopher (auto + St. Christopher, the patron saint of travelers). Some older people still called it the "Useless Carriage," but the newspapers finally dropped the hyphen and settled on "automobile."

By the summer of 1899, many people who had never dreamed of giving up their horses came down with "automobile fever." Store windows displayed "touring outfits." For men there were light summer suits, covered with long linen dusters that reached to their heels, a yachting cap, cotton gloves, and immense blue wire goggles. Women's outfits were long linen dusters and huge hats with "dust veils" that wrapped completely around the head and face. Soon fashion designers were working on the ultimate "touring outfit," because the new "sport" of automobiling required a special uniform of its own. Magazines began appearing especially for automobilists. Even advertisements for something not even related to automobiles could not resist mentioning the new craze:

> AN AUTOMOBILE
> will soon become the most convenient conveyance.
> But while it will contribute to everyone's comfort
> it will not be so essential for mankind as the use of
> Johann Hoff's Malt Extract
> for building up a weakened constitution.

Still, most young people in the United States had never seen an automobile. Autos rarely left the paved streets of the cities, because roads were so terrible. Through 1902, when a country person had a ride in the newfangled automobile, the occasion was so special that his or her name usually appeared in the following week's newspaper. Besides wealthy people, doctors were almost the only others who had the money to buy autos. Doctors found them hard to resist for late-night calls.

When a person made the big decision to buy a car, he usually hired a "chauffeur" to go with it and keep it polished and in good shape. This is the way things were done in Europe, where automobiles were no longer the novelty they were in the United States. However, the owners found that many American chauffeurs knew very little more about the inner workings of the machine than they did themselves.

As for what to do with the automobile, now that it was here, no one except a doctor was quite sure. The wealthy young men wanted to get out on the roads and race against other makes of cars. Some men collected their families for a "motor pic-nic" in the country. But the Sunday after-church parade along the boulevard was out, because the noisy motors frightened the horse carriages, making the new motorcar owners very unpopular.

On the Road

At seven on the morning of Monday, May 22, 1899, Alexander Winton decided to show people what they could do with an automobile. He was president of the Winton Motor Carriage Manufacturing Company in Cleveland, Ohio. Gasoline motors had advantages over the electric autos, and Winton planned to show one of them. He and a newspaperman, Charles B. Shanks, set off on the first long-distance, "high speed" auto trip to New York, over seven hundred miles away. The high speed the pair reached was an average of 17½ miles an hour—but that was almost twice as fast as a horse. Unfortu-

A bicycle-mounted policeman pinches a speeder

nately the roads were more suited to horses.

"We ran over an embankment and broke the front axle in two," said Winton. But he didn't give up. He telegraphed the company for a new axle, laid over until it was replaced, and started off again. They reached the Astor Hotel in New York just before dinner on Friday.

"Some of the roads between Buffalo and Albany," said Winton angrily, "would be discreditable in Middle Africa."

"What was your fastest speed?" a reporter asked.

"Twenty miles an hour is fast enough for anyone," Winton

answered. "At 35 miles per hour, a person can hardly keep his seat in the carriage."

The first cars sat on hard high wheels, and a driver felt that he was teetering at the edge of a diving board. He looked straight down onto the road; not even a windshield was there to slow him down if the car hit a bump. Most cars did not even have sides for a person to lean against when going around a corner.

The roads were so terrible that new drivers could hardly wait to take their autos onto the attractive roads of Central Park in New York or the park in Chicago. This caught park commissioners off guard, and they all uttered a horrified *"No!"*

Four teenagers, one sitting on the running board wearing driving goggles, try out Jim's new Pierce Arrow

They were supported by the horse-carriage owners, who greatly outnumbered the automobile owners. One Chicago man was arrested for driving his electric auto with quiet cushioned tires along Michigan Avenue. The police said he was "disturbing the peace," even though he hadn't made a sound. A New York man who tried to drive in Central Park was arrested because he might frighten a horse if he went near one, and besides, said the police, his car was "a disfigurement on the landscape."

In Newport, Rhode Island, where the wealthy auto owners went for their summer fun, the golf courses were almost empty. Golf had taken over from bicycling as the newest sport the summer before. Now the old horse barns at Newport were being used to store automobiles which wealthy vacationers could rent by the hour and learn to drive. The big cities were going to be invaded, come fall, by an army of "new drivers."

Automobiles brought problems that city officials and police had never dreamed of. They had regulated the speed at which a horse carriage could move on a city street, but no rules were ready for the new kind of drivers. The city police were all mounted—on bicycles.

One July evening, James Donahue was sitting in his new automobile in front of Grand Central Station looking for something exciting to do.

"There's a gentleman at the Union Square Hotel who wants to catch the 8:20 express," he heard one electric cab driver tell another. "Says it's worth $5 to him."

"Could never make it," said the other. "It's 8:05 now."

"I can do it!" shouted Donahue, delighted at the idea of a race without competitors. He opened the lever of his car so fast and wide that the machine jumped forward, almost throwing him out of his seat. Donahue swung into 42nd Street on two wheels, almost turning over, and raced at the highest speed he could muster down Fifth Avenue. He kept one foot on the bells, ringing constantly to get traffic out of his way. But the street was filled with carriages and wheelmen on bicycles out for their evening spin. Twisting in and out, Donahue shook up one bicyclist after another, unseating them from their wheels and leaving them shaking fists in rage.

At 34th Street, he roared downhill close to thirty-five miles an hour, according to several eyewitnesses. When he hit the trolley car tracks, the car bounced six inches into the air.

Bicycle policeman Dobson claimed later that he heard Donahue's car coming toward him at 28th Street "like the roar of a small tornado." He mounted his wheel and gave chase. Six blocks later, Donahue had to slow down because of the traffic, and there Dobson caught up with him.

"You're under arrest," Dobson shouted over the traffic noise.

"But I have a passenger to get—he wants to catch the 8:20 train," said Donahue, truly surprised that a policeman could be so contrary. But Dobson hauled him off to the police station without further ado. There the sergeant informed him that it was too bad he hadn't been riding a bicycle, because the law allowed wheelmen to leave their wheels inside the station for security when they were arrested, and leave until time for their hearing. Since Donahue could not leave his wheels there, he had to stay in a cell instead.

That same week, in July 1899, John and Louise Davis shocked people by starting "for the West Coast" in their Duryea touring car. No one had ever actually planned to drive to the West Coast, and even the Davises had no idea whether they could find any roads.

"Well, we'll follow the covered wagon trails . . . or drive along the railroad tracks . . . or something," she told reporters. Mr. Davis said very little. The Davis car had a horseshoe hung on the radiator, not only for good luck, but to show they did not have any grudges against horses.

Like most automobiles of that year, the Davis car had no solid roof, but they had added a folding "buggy-type" roof to cover them from rain. Isinglass curtains rolled down for added protection. The Davises had no idea what they were getting into.

Thursday, July 13, the Davises left from the Herald Building at 34th and Broadway in New York, amid cheers and Indian whoops of the many young boys gathered to watch the excitement. A long row of automobiles followed the pair up Fifth Avenue as far as the Harlem River.

For the next few days, people eagerly watched the newspapers for reports of the "venturesome tourists," as they conquered one problem after another. By the second day Mr. Davis had hired a mechanic at Peekskill, New York, who agreed to go with them as far as Buffalo.

"Our problems are because the car is just out of the shop," Davis explained with embarrassment. "As soon as it is worn

down to the bearings, it will work all right."

Leaving Peekskill, after repairs, several wheelmen followed the Duryea to see what would happen when it reached Nelson Hill. No car yet had been able to climb up the Hill. But the Davises shot up over the hill in fine style. They were so excited that they took a wrong turn and got lost. That night crowds of people waiting to see them at Poughkeepsie escorted them into town and to the nearest repair garage.

The Davises struggled through twenty-five major breakdowns. Finally, on August 19, they reached Detroit and decided to give up. By that time there was hardly an original piece left in the machine. They were not the only family who did not reach the West Coast. No one succeeded before 1903.

What's an Auto For?

What to do with the automobile became a new guessing game in 1900. The newspapers reported each bright idea as it came along. In Buffalo, autos were used to collect the mails, and the post office department said they took only half as much time as horses. The express company used an auto as an express wagon. The Baltimore and Ohio used an auto to carry passengers to and from the railroad station. In Akron, Ohio, the police used one as a patrol wagon. A mover in Cleveland used an auto to move a piano. One man in Ashtabula, Ohio, said an auto made a perfect plow. A passing train had set his fields on fire, and the only way he could save them was to plow a quick furrow between the burning wheat and the rest of his field. No one was home to help, so he hooked the plow to his automobile, and it worked.

Doctors were the first to convince hospitals to use automobiles for ambulances. An electric ambulance could travel fast for a longer time than a horse. Besides, when it arrived at the

The automobile ambulance had many advantages over a horse-pulled one

hospital, there was no need to care for the steaming horse as well as for the patient. No time was lost hitching up. The electric car was charged up when it was not being used, and it could be kept near the hospital, because there were no "stable odors" to infect the hospital patients.

The First Horseless Horse Show

New York society people loved dressing up for special shows. The Horse Show and the Bicycle Show had always brought them out in their finery to Madison Square Garden. In 1900, the big show was entirely given over to the new sport of automobiling. The first show of the Automobile Club of America opened on November 4.

The club had decorated the Garden with American flags, bunting, and draperies. At the center of each group of drapes was a large rubber-tired automobile wheel. "Automobile red" lamps were everywhere. In the middle of the floor was a twenty-foot track of wood. In its center, covered with tanbark from the horse show, were shiny automobiles. Platforms had been built over the box seats to hold more automobiles from the seventy companies that had sent exhibits. A bridge led across the wooden track, and people lined up on it to take their turns at free auto rides. Even the restaurant was filled "with vehicles that go by themselves." The food had been moved upstairs to the concert hall, but few people were interested in eating.

The Automobile Club had sponsored several "runs" during the summer. They were not meant to be races, but few of the drivers could resist trying to beat the automobiles owned by their friends. By the summer's end, those who attended the "runs" had improved their own driving. They had climbed hills they had not thought possible and learned much about their automobiles. They had raced steam, electric, and gasoline-powered autos against each other and learned the weak and strong points of each kind of motor. Society ladies had planned "chauffeur" and "automobile" parties, taking off from home with the utmost confidence that their hired chauffeurs would be able to get them all back safely before dark. Thousands of people who did not even know what a motor car was a year before were now geared up to attend the first automobile show.

The crowds were even larger than the Automobile Club had hoped, but the society people held off, as they always had for the horse shows, until the second or third day. The first days the show was packed with people who did not look as if they could afford to buy an automobile, and the salesmen were discouraged. But these people had been doing some figuring.

Not counting the initial expense, an automobile was actually cheaper to keep than a horse. A horse cost $115 to buy. With its feed, cost of a license, and shoeing, the total expense of keeping a horse for a year came to $159. Meanwhile, a five-horsepower car (equal, in some people's minds, to five horses) cost $850 plus a tax of $21. Fuel cost about 75 cents to travel

STUDEBAKER

"THE AUTOMOBILE WITH A REPUTATION BEHIND IT."

WITH an eye to long-continued usefulness, the careful purchaser will appreciate the value of Studebaker design, materials and workmanship. Even were other considerations equal, the comfort, elegance and DURABILITY of Studebaker Automobiles guarantee unequaled satisfaction. Our agents will gladly give further particulars, or catalogues will be sent on request.

THE STUDEBAKER ELECTRIC CAR

has been thoroughly tested by actual use, and the fact that we are constantly receiving orders to duplicate shipments proves that it is eminently satisfactory as a convenient, easily-run automobile for local use. Equipped with Edison or Exide batteries and made in a variety of types.

THE STUDEBAKER GASOLENE TOURING CAR

is designed for long-distance touring. It is a light, noiseless and powerful car, which incorporates the most modern improvements. Made by a concern whose name is a synonym for reliability, and sold at a price which makes it an unusually profitable purchase.

STUDEBAKER AUTOMOBILE CO., - SOUTH BEND, IND.

BRANCH HOUSES:

NEW YORK CITY: Broadway, corner 48th Street.
CHICAGO, ILL.: 378-388 Wabash Avenue.
KANSAS CITY, MO.: 810-814 Walnut Street.
SAN FRANCISCO, CAL.: Corner Market and 10th Streets.
PORTLAND, ORE.: 330-334 East Morrison Street.
DENVER, COL.: Corner 15th and Blake Streets.
SALT LAKE CITY, UTAH: 157-159 State Street.
DALLAS, TEX.: 317-319 Elm Street.

AGENCIES IN OTHER PRINCIPAL CITIES.

AUTOMOBILES

Even a woman can drive, says this Studebaker ad, with one hand free to hold her hat

35 miles, and a car could travel a hundred miles on nine gallons of gasoline on good roads. This brought the cost of keeping a car for a year to only $111.25.

The show had an unbelievable array of automobiles, delivery trucks, heavy trucks, Victorias, and broughams. The café and main corridor were filled with famous French racing machines, but races never caught on in the United States in quite the same way they had in France. The crowd also saw a copy of Richard Dudgeon's 1855 steam carriage, which had been lost in the Crystal Palace fire. Dudgeon's carriage looked like an iron locomotive next to the sleek metal bodies of the "modern" autos.

Each evening eager people waited their turn for a ride around the wooden track. For many it was their first and probably their only chance to ride until automobile prices became cheaper.

"Society night" finally came, and the Astors, Vanderbilts, Rockefellers, Van Rensselaers, and others showed up in full tuxedo, furs, and diamonds. In addition to the sounds of the horseless carriages inside, a band played marches and strong voices sang operatic arias. John Jacob Astor announced that he had driven ninety miles to the show—and had averaged 18 miles an hour. Sidney D. Ripley was impressed, but he had a racing man's instinct. He left the show early with two friends. An hour later he telephoned to Madison Square Garden, and the master of ceremonies announced that he had covered the ground to his home at an average of 25 miles an hour.

In addition to watching each other, the crowd that night watched an obstacle race for electric autos. The humming cars circled the wooden track, dodging fences, boxes, barrels, and people. Later in the evening, everyone took turns driving the electric cars around the track. One woman driver caused a stir among envious women, who called her "a bold one," but se-

The "Automobile Girl" chose her driving clothes carefully so the breeze would not expose her ankles cretly planned to include driving an auto in their futures.

The next day the pace slowed down. The society folk had gone off to the steeplechase at Meadowbrook, and it was election day. Business picked up, though, when the show managers thought up some novel ideas for the remaining days. People with money came back to see the fun and stayed to buy. One man bought his family an electric Victoria with pearl gray lining and cushions, and uniforms to match for the groom and chauffeur. Apparently it never occurred to him that an auto needed no groom. Another bought a $2,500 white enamel open car with pigskin cushions and a golf bag attached to the rear seat.

Among the novel ideas was a braking contest to see which cars could stop in the shortest distance without throwing the driver out of his seat. Gasoline engine cars had an obstacle race —making far more noise and smell than the electric cars. Salesmen kept telling electric car fanciers that soon every little village would have an "electrant"—a sort of hydrant that would give an electric car a 25-mile "charge" for a quarter. (Electric car owners were always worried that they would run out of power before they made it home again.) There were delivery wagon races and a rousing steam tricycle race. Each driver of a steam tricycle took a running start at the sound of the pistol, jumped aboard his three-wheeled car, and took off. The rule included stopping at the 40-yard line to remove his coat and hang it on a tree, then he jumped back in and pulled open the valve for speed. At the next stop each man had to unbutton his vest and drive around the track to where his coat was. By this time the crowd was joining in the fun. The men wore pink, blue, and yellow shirts—that alone was hilarious to the audience of white-shirted men. The pink-shirted man stopped so suddenly that his car turned completely around by itself. The men dashed around the track, rebuttoning their vests and coats and racing for the finish line as the crowd roared approval.

Over ten thousand people saw the first auto show, and not one of them doubted that the automobile was here to stay.

Electric, Steam, or Gasoline?

At first the electric automobiles looked the best. Women weren't afraid of them, and they ran with the quietest humming sound. But they were slow—even slower on a cold day. The battery had to be charged all night for use the next day. The driver kept finding ways to save the battery, by coasting to a stop or coasting downhill with the current switched off. Electric cars had the worst reputations for going uphill. They were almost impossible on a long trip, even though, a year after the auto show, they could go forty miles without a charge. The West was never going to be settled by electric cars.

Automobiles with steam engines were very touchy to start. The driver had to pump up the pressure, light a fire under a boiler and wait for the steam pressure to rise. One tank of water was enough to make steam for fifty miles. When that ran out, the driver just helped himself to water from a stream or the nearest horse's trough, but dirty water was likely to gum up the boiler. To climb a hill, the driver had to get the steam up to about five hundred pounds pressure. The excess steam then had to be let off, making an earsplitting roar. In 1902, one driver climbed up a high mountain and just at the top met a stagecoach filled with passengers. When he let off the excess steam, the horses took fright and jumped over the edge of the road, dragging the stagecoach and screaming passengers down the mountainside. This sort of behavior made it hard for steam auto drivers to make friends on the road.

Most steam car owners bragged that their cars were most

likely to get them home, even when they needed repairs. But the cars were very light, and few people thought of them as long-distance cars.

That left only gasoline engine cars to help settle the western states. The gas engines had much against them from the start. They were too noisy for well-bred people to admire, although the men liked racing them. And then there was the shortage of gasoline. The Standard Oil Company, in 1905, was concerned about a shortage if the automobile makers continued building gasoline autos at their present rate. Officials announced that they would have to raise their prices. There were no gasoline stations. The only place a traveler could buy gasoline in a strange town was in a repair garage. If desperate, he could sometimes buy a few pints in a drugstore. Most drivers carried extra cans of gasoline with them. Still the gasoline engine looked as though it was the only one that could carry an automobile across the country.

"You will have the feeling of being lifted up and carried away," the salesman told his prospective buyer. "You'll never feel pulled or pushed again."

Partly because of the salesman's description and partly because of the shiny paint of the auto, another American citizen bought a car in the early 1900s. He had no idea how to drive it, but the salesman assured him there would be no problems. The company's chauffeur would deliver it to his garage that very evening.

Sometimes a buyer went to an automobile shop in the morning and drove his own car home that night. A mechanic showed him how to steer with the lever (the first cars had tillers, rather like sailboats, instead of a steering wheel), and how to work the hand and foot brake. The power (speed) was controlled with another lever. If he got the levers mixed up, he was in trouble. Usually the mechanic sent the buyer and his new car out into a field until the owner got the hang of turning on the power slowly. One fast movement and the car was likely to bolt over curbs or do a swift about-face.

"If it doesn't work, I can always call the factory," the new owner told himself. Automobile factory mechanics had a large collection of stories about new drivers who called from some town miles away or telegraphed from the nearest railroad station if they could not find a telephone. Hours later a weary mechanic would arrive on the scene, only to find the gas tank empty.

Part of learning to drive was learning how to take care of the automobile in the winter. Not only were the roads worse in winter, but in a northern climate it was just too cold to use an automobile which had no top, sides, or doors. In the winter, the auto owner took off all the loose parts—the horn, lamps, picnic baskets, and floor mats, and he disconnected the battery. He emptied and cleaned the lamps. Then he removed the tires and jacked up the body, cleaning every inch of the shiny paint. He wrapped the tires tenderly in cloth and put them away. Then he emptied the water and gas tanks and drained the oil. Taking off the wheels, he cleaned and oiled them. A steam car also had to have the boiler thoroughly cleaned.

While waiting for spring, the auto driver subscribed to one of the new auto magazines and read about his favorite new sport. *Outing* magazine listed some of the emergencies the new driver might meet and told him how to cope with them.

"What would you do if . . ." began the article.

". . . if a flock of pigeons should fly up suddenly in your face?" If it's too late to slow down for the pigeons or chickens, you were told, then duck (keeping at least one eye on the road), throw your arm over your head, and steer for the center of the road. There was no windshield or even a motor in front to protect the driver. A flock of birds in the face not only hurt, but filled the air with dust and feathers.

". . . if a cow wanders onto the road?" Cows are stupid and move in the way you least expect them to, the article said. They are also big. Always slow down for a cow.

". . . if a woman steps off a street curb in front of you?" Don't blow your horn, the article warned, because "women frighten easily in city streets and often behave like a cow. Drive slowly through cities."

". . . if a dog runs in front of the car?" If you cannot get out of the dog's way, then run over it—unless it's a very large dog. In that case grip the controls very firmly as there is going to be a big bump. Cars were so high off the road that often the dog was not hurt, but drivers did not carry bumper stickers that said "I brake for animals." Instead drivers were advised to carry cigars to help settle arguments with owners of chickens and dogs.

". . . if you want to pass a car going in the same direction?" The driver could never see ahead, because the car in front usually raised so much dust in his face. "The time to pass," said the article, "is when you notice the dust cloud is close to the ground and you feel it beating against your face from below. Then blow your horn continually, pull over as far to the left as you can, and trust to your luck. . . . If someone else is coming, you will not have time to arrange any little matters before the funeral."

". . . if the brakes don't work when you are going down a mountain road?" If the car should run away, the driver was told, steer into a bank or a tree "without killing yourself." As a last resort, said the article, throw the car into reverse gear. This ruins the machinery, but that can be fixed easier than a broken skull. Autos then had both hand and foot brakes, but neither was always sure to work. They heated up when climbing or descending hills and had to be used one at a time.

". . . if the car begins to coast backwards going up a steep grade?" Brakes did not hold when the car started backward. A foreign car had a sort of pick that dropped down under the car and held it like an anchor until it could move forward again. But the driver of an American car had to shift into the lowest gear and use the slow forward motion to hold the car at rest.

"The whole question of meeting emergencies lies in having an alert mind," says *Outing* magazine, confident that the new driver was now prepared to meet every emergency that would come his way in the spring.

The Brogan Method of Driving

"My first motor car had just arrived and been safely placed in the barn by the company's chauffeur," said William G. Brogan of Buffalo one April day in 1905. "It was a beauty—a symphony in colors, and had all the latest improvements—four cylinders, side entrance, and all."

Brogan's best friends, Fred and Jack, were only too happy to help him enjoy it. The boys decided the best way to learn how to drive it would be to tour from home to Niagara Falls, twenty miles away. Brogan had read every catalog on driving that he could find, but he still was not sure he could make the round trip of forty miles.

"Why not? It's perfectly simple," said Fred, who knew nothing at all about driving.

"A lot of green hands have turned into full-fledged drivers after just one trip into the country," said Jack with perfect assurance.

Brogan finally agreed, but he still spent all evening studying a book of instructions. When he finally fell asleep, he dreamed of clutches, gears, tire patches, and carburetors.

"I arose bright and early," said Brogan. "When a single turn of the crank started the hum of the engine, I became exceedingly confident. I climbed into the seat, seized the steering wheel, let in the clutch, and rolled through the barn door—but with more speed than seemed absolutely necessary. Since then, I have wondered what would have been the result if the barn door had been half an inch narrower, for, as I glided through the opening I had just time to notice that the door jamb was scraping the paint off the edge of the mud guard. I went safely through, however, and had a straight and clear road to the street.

"Through a mistaken notion that the steering wheel worked on the principle of the wheel of a ship, and that it should be turned in the opposite direction to that in which I wanted to go, I headed up the street instead of down. In the surprise and confusion of this unexpected turn of affairs, I mounted the curb on a return trip to the barn by way of the lawn and front porch before reason asserted itself. A turn of the wheel in the proper direction carried me over the curb and into the street again, but at such an abrupt angle that I narrowly escaped colliding with a tree in front of my neighbor's house."

Since he should have headed south instead of north to pick up Fred and Jack, Brogan thought he would go around the block. He decided against turning in the street because it looked much narrower than he had ever noticed.

"Getting around the first corner safely, I felt more at ease and advanced the speed lever, which was a mistake. Because of the increased speed of the car, I narrowly escaped contact with a lamp post at my next turn. Fortune favored, though, and, owing to a premature release of the clutch—under the idea that the car would run several hundred feet on its own momentum—I got within five houses of the desired spot and rolled on by."

Jack and Fred ran shouting after him. They thought the auto was running away with Brogan, and they would miss the fun if they didn't run to catch him. But the car stopped several houses beyond, and they jumped in. When Brogan started up again he forgot to put the car in first gear. With a lunge forward, the motor stopped dead. Fred cranked the engine to restart it, but since he didn't know the proper position to stand in, the crank kicked back and landed a blow on his arm.

"Having started the engine, while Fred nursed his arm and said things, we proceeded in the direction of Delaware Avenue at a rate of about twenty-five miles an hour, narrowly avoiding running into the rear of a trolley car and the side of a milk wagon. Emerging on that beautiful avenue with a confidence born of ignorance, I advanced the speed lever several notches, and we rolled along rapidly."

Luckily no automobiles came out of the cross streets, because Brogan was still slow at finding the brake. He sped down one hill only to have the engine slow gradually and finally stop as he climbed another hill. The machine began slowly to back down the hill.

"My emotions veered to panic. Recovering sufficiently to throw on the hub brakes, I was relieved to feel the car slow down and then stop. Descending, I cranked the engine, took my seat, and let in the clutch. There was a terrible vibration and the motor stopped again. Remembering that 'the low gear always should be used in starting,' I threw the lever to that position, and tried again but without result. It then dawned on me that the tightly-locked brakes on the rear hubs had something to do with the difficulty. Upon again starting the engine, releasing the brake lever, and letting in the clutch, the car started and climbed slowly but surely to the top of the hill."

Farther along, the road was mostly filled with the high T-rails of the trolley track. The big yellow trolleys traveled along it as fast as a railroad train and only fifteen minutes apart. Brogan straddled the tracks until the trolleys came along. He had to swerve frequently to let them pass.

"It was along here that I learned of that eccentricity of the chicken family which every motorist knows. I had noticed a brood of chickens at one side of the road, and was startled to see them try to cross in front of the machine just as we reached them, under the apparent idea that safety lay only on the other side. Being tenderhearted and having visions of an irate farmer and damages as well, I swerved from my path into the ditch and bumped along in the mud and water for several rods before it again occurred to me to return to the road.

"After this incident, it struck me that both Fred and Jack were strangely quiet, and it gradually dawned on me with pain that their confidence in my ability to meet the emergencies which beset the motorist's path was waning. I really felt hurt, for I considered that I was doing well, having in the brief space of an hour narrowly avoided several mishaps which might have proven quite serious."

In spite of his friends' distrust, Brogan was beginning to feel very confident. He even considered pushing the lever up to the highest notch of speed, when he suddenly noticed two trolley cars coming toward him from opposite directions. Their rate of speed was sure to bring them and Brogan's auto together at the same spot in the road. The space to the right of the trolley tracks was being excavated for a sewer. He had to decide on some course quickly.

"I crossed over both tracks between the cars when they were about a hundred feet apart, bumped through a hole several feet deep, narrowly avoided a trolley pole, and rolled on serenely with renewed confidence as the trolleys whizzed by."

After dinner at Niagara Falls, the boys decided to run down to Devil's Hole below the suspension bridge. Brogan tried to save the tires by avoiding the stones along the country road, but managed to hit most of them as well as those lying harmlessly along both sides of the road.

"Here the most thrilling experience of the day occurred. Trying to avoid a rather deep rut, I turned too far and ran off the road and up a straight incline on the grass above. This would not have been serious, but the road at this point was perilously close to the river. We were not aware of that until we caught beside us a momentary glimpse of the seething whirlpool 200 feet or more below us as we rapidly rolled to within a few feet of the edge of the cliff."

Jack and Fred shrieked. Brogan somehow turned the wheel quickly, and they headed once more for the road.

"I'm taking the trolley back to the Falls," said Jack. "You can pick me up on your way home."

But Fred and Brogan managed to calm him. Soon it was five o'clock, and the boys decided to have supper at the Falls before taking a moonlight ride home. Just then the engine stopped again.

Brogan got out the instruction book. He asked Fred to check the gasoline tank, but Fred said it was half full. Brogan cleaned, tested, and replaced the spark plugs, but still there was no life in the engine. Then Brogan checked the gas tank. Fred had mistaken the shiny bottom of the tank for gasoline. He was sent off on the trolley to the Falls to buy a can of fuel. By the time Fred returned and the boys had eaten supper, the night was as black as a deep cave.

"It was too dark to see the road, for the moon failed to come out. I was greatly surprised to notice that all the stones and ruts which I had mentally marked for future guidance on the down trip had disappeared, and the road, to all appearances, was perfectly smooth and level. A rear tire flattened, but we got that into shape after an hour's work. We also stopped on the railroad track at La Salle, owing to an excess of caution in crossing too slowly."

Fred and Jack leaped out and pushed the auto off the track before a train came. The boys finally reached home just after midnight.

"For stimulating nerve action, there is nothing like a motor trip conducted by a green operator," said Jack.

"However," said Brogan, "we all agreed we knew more than when we started, and that our motoring education is now fairly under way."

Autos, Women, and Clothes

From the earliest days women had sensed that automobiling was a sport that would include them. Every time the ladies got behind the wheel, the newspapers noticed them. When the Central Park commissioners finally decided to allow automobiles in the park, hundreds of drivers took tests to show their ability. Florence Wood, a seventeen-year-old, was the first woman to be allowed to drive there. The commissioner, who was supposed to give her a test, was leery of women drivers, so he sent out his secretary instead, and Florence passed with flying colors. She drove her auto to school every day in New York.

"An automobile is the easiest thing in the world to handle," she told newspapermen. "Any girl could operate an auto as easily as she could drive a pony."

Another lady shocked women by driving alone forty-five miles into Cleveland, Ohio, to do her shopping. Mrs. Clarence Mackay made headlines in 1905 because she had a car with a roof and "glass sides." Women envied her because she didn't have to wear "swaddling veils or billowing ulster" as they did in open automobiles.

By spring 1905, "the motor girl" had become an important part of the landscape. Many Easter gifts for a lady that year were automobile-oriented. A man sent his girl violets or lilies of the valley in a little wicker motorcar or in a flower box decorated with colorful motorcars and a lady with her veil blowing. He might choose a tiny motorcar with rubber wheels filled with bonbons or buy her a silk rubber dust protector to wear over her Easter clothes. In jewelry there was a long safety motor hatpin which was an enameled dragonfly with matching dragonflies to pin down her veil. The most expensive gift was a diamond brooch in the shape of a car with a tiny watch in the wheel.

Women were always being told they made terrible drivers and that they did not "take naturally to driving" as men did. Yet there were not so many accidents caused by women as by men drivers.

"The only thing about a car that a woman doesn't have to learn," said a 1904 magazine, "is how to dress for it."

Instead of automobiles being closed up to protect the driver and the riders, people wore all their protection. The man wore an automobile cap, which looked just like a yachting cap. It covered his head and stayed on tight when the wind blew. A long face mask and goggles protected his face from small stones and flying insects which could hit with stinging force. He wore gauntlets (fleece-lined in cold weather) with wide cuffs that covered his coat sleeves. In spring, a man bought a long, light leather coat that was soft and waterproof and cost about thirty-five dollars. For winter a man bought a long, heavy mackintosh. Unless the hem was lined with heavy leather, his long coat blew up over his knees when he drove fast or it got tangled around the gears. On a hot summer day, a man could be well dressed in a khaki suit with leather leggings.

Ladies also wore long coats hemmed with leather to keep them anchored down and hide their ankles. A lady wore a cheviot cloth duster, with a pleat down the back so she could move her shoulders and with several pockets to hold such items as her face mask and goggles. Ladies never wore the comfortable yachting caps that men wore, because the ladies were supposed to wear large hats. Large hats did not work at all in automobiles, and yet the ladies wrapped veils around and around, trying desperately to hold them on. A straw hat "with a detachable curtain" was the most sensible kind of hat allowed for a woman, until finally some women began wearing large berets that stayed on fairly well. It was unthinkable for a woman to appear outside her home without a hat covering her head. A hat was almost essential to hold down the long, intricate hairdos that were the style. Short hair was not acceptable until about ten years later.

When a lady went on a simple picnic, in the early 1900s, looking "right" was important. She packed a long scarf, veil, hairpins, hairnet, and a vanity case with toilet accessories, comb, brush, mirror, powder puffs, powder boxes, alcohol lamp, curling iron, jar of cold cream, an extra handkerchief or two, and a hatpin case filled with pins of various sizes.

Rules and Races

One of the first discoveries a new automobile owner made was that he could no longer drink and be sure to get home safely. In the old days, even if his own head were muddled, he could always count on his horse being sober and taking him home without accident—sometimes even with the driver asleep. This no longer worked in an auto. Now that man rather than horse was in charge, the highways and back roads needed new rules and laws.

At first, automobile rules were set locally. When a farmer complained that autos had blown dust all over his strawberries, the local sheriff set the speed limit at no faster than a horse walks. The sheriff did not always put up a sign to warn drivers about the speed limit.

Some rules were confusing, like those for passing other vehicles on the road. Motorists hated coming up behind a horse and wagon and having to follow in the dust rather than pass to the clean air and clear road ahead. A wagon driver passed another team on the *right,* but an auto driver was supposed to pass on the *left.* Most roads were only one lane wide where they crossed a bridge. Aggressive drivers approached a bridge blowing horns wildly to warn oncoming cars that they had first claim to the one-lane bridge. No signs warned drivers what was ahead on the road—deep ditches, dangerous dips that might fill with water after a rain, or winding roads. The Automobile Club tried to settle some of the confusion.

In 1905, the first rules of the road were published. All vehicles must drive on the right side of a public highway. A driver should signal with his hand straight up if he intended to stop. Motorists were not to blow their horns at horses. Oil lamp headlights must be lit an hour before sunset. A driver was not to run away after running down someone. And a strict no-no was oiling your license plate and throwing dust on it so it could not be read.

Because rules differed from one village to another, the Automobile Club tried to warn drivers where its members felt that tickets were being handed out unfairly.

"Be careful at Good Ground on the South Shore Road of Long Island," the club warned, "especially on Saturdays or Sundays. A member reports that any car is held up that can be boarded and fined $25, the officer being most insolent."

"At Sag Harbor they stop speeders with a rope."

"Central Valley and Highland Mills, Orange County, New Jersey, insist upon automobiles not going over ten miles per hour. There is a decided hostility to automobilists in these two towns," reported the Automobile Club.

Especially hard on cross-country drivers were the contrary rules in different states. In Michigan a motorist could drive 15 miles an hour in the city and 25 out in the country. But in Missouri, a motorist discovered, usually after paying a large fine, that he was supposed to drive only 9 miles an hour everywhere in that state. Besides this, he had to pay a two-dollar fee to every county he drove through in Missouri and ten dollars more for the privilege of driving in the city of St. Louis. To make matters worse, the local constable could fine a driver the minute he drove over the county line for not having his "license" for that county, even though he could not possibly get a license before he reached the county seat to buy it.

The American newspapers reported the news about racing motorcars in Europe, but Americans had too many other ideas for automobiles. The few races and contests held in this country were not so much for competition as they were for improvement of the machines and the drivers.

Hill-climbing contests were popular, because every driver knew that a single hill could keep him from going where he wanted. Every year a large contest was held at Eagle Rock Hill in Orange, New Jersey. Sometimes the cars were divided by their costs, and this was a revelation to potential auto buyers. The most expensive cars were not always best on the hills. In 1904, no one was surprised that the two fastest cars were a 60-horsepower Renault racer and a 90-horsepower Mercedes, but they were surprised to see an Oldsmobile that cost under $850 and a $1,000 Buick win races against cars that cost three times as much money.

Reliability tests were not only a way to judge which make of

Camping in Yellowstone Park was very informal in 1920

car was the best, but a way to make the manufacturers improve their models. Only half the cars that began a New York to Rochester race in 1901 were able to finish. One year later, 78 cars raced from New York to Boston, and only nine failed to finish the two-day event. Automobiles were improving.

Automobile Touring

Most people saw automobiling as a sport with three branches: racing, touring, and (for plucky people) camping. Racing never caught on here as it had in Europe, and camping was pretty much for hunters and fishermen, not ladies. But touring—there was a sport for all Americans.

By 1902, automobile makers had dropped some of the racing features and concentrated on making their cars with lower bodies, a longer wheelbase, and stronger wheels. There was more space for feet and luggage. Taking the family on a trip by automobile was like having a railroad coach all to oneself.

Vacations were still a revolutionary idea to some people. Russell Sage was one who felt that no man needed a vacation.

"The vacation habit is the outgrowth of distorted business methods," said Sage, wondering, at the same time, why he had such a hard time keeping his employees. "I would not dream of asking my employer for time off—that is time which belongs to him and that he has paid for. It's ridiculous that a man who works 11½ months can't work for 12 months."

Evidently not everyone agreed with Sage, because men were now asking their bosses for a two-week summer vacation and hinting that they also would like an occasional Saturday free as well. The men who could afford to buy the earliest

The AAA driver and dog head down the "highway" toward the Wayside Inn for the night

automobiles could afford to take Saturday off.

Sometimes they planned a day's tour with the family, and stopped at a historic inn for supper before the final run home to the city. When this happened, motor travelers were always shocked to find that innkeepers had not changed much since the days of stagecoaches. One family, after driving all day without much to eat, arrived at a hundred-year-old inn about 5 P.M. They had just time to eat quickly and reach New York City before dark.

"Dinner will be served at 6:30," the landlord protested.

After their many pleas and promises to pay a little extra, the landlord finally agreed that he could move the dinner hour forward to 6:00 P.M. for his starving tourists. But he must have forgotten to tell the cook, because the meal was not ready at six. The landlord was a man who kept up appearances, however. He set the clock back to 5:30, and when it struck six the meal was served.

At country inns, travelers ate with all sorts of dining partners, but they did not pay the same prices. When a farmer drove in with his load of vegetables for market, he was served in the dining room and charged 25 cents, even though he might eat as much as three men. A commercial man, sitting at the same table, was charged 50 cents and the bicyclist 75 cents for the same meal. The motorist invariably had to pay a dollar.

One of the niceties of touring was a wicker basket, called a "motor hamper," which sometimes came as one of the automobile's accessories. Hampers usually included a "cold" compartment as well as an alcohol lamp to heat up hot drinks or food. Ice went in the lowest tier, next came the lunch, and on top, within easy reach, were plates, cups, and utensils, all strapped into place.

Touring could mean any length of trip—from one day to several days. Drivers delighted in telling each other how they had solved problems along the road where there was no help to be found. They shared one miserable fact—the roads were unbearable!

One motorist claimed that the mud of North Carolina roads would put molasses to shame. What worked in one kind of mud did not necessarily work in another kind of mud. What was the best way to go down a steep and muddy hill? One driver cut off a large tree branch and dragged it behind his car as an anchor. How can you cross a stream where there is no bridge? One motorist borrowed the railroad ties from a nearby train track in Wyoming and built himself a bridge.

Sometimes the problems of motorists were not *with* the roads but because the motorists went *without* roads. The great fun in touring was that a driver could go anywhere his car would take him. He was not limited to a road as a railroad car was to a track. Edward Ayer started across the desert country around California's Imperial Valley with his wife, maid, and chauffeur one day.

"It was impossible to get across the great sand dunes," said Ayer disgustedly, "until we got about forty to forty-five miles north of what is called the Grand Wash. Autos sometimes came through the sand there with great difficulty."

Ayer, his wife, the chauffeur, and the maid pulled up brush and grass to try to make a "road" in the sand so the wheels could get some traction. They moved five miles in the same number of hours. Finally, with the chauffeur digging the wheels out, they moved fifty feet before bogging down again. By night they reached a town and found a place to sleep.

Next morning Ayer asked the way to El Centro, sixteen miles away.

"It's a sea of mud," said a man from town. "Water spout flooded the valley yesterday."

At last Ayer found a man who took $20 to lead them on a

forty-mile detour around the water.

"At nine in the morning he put us into a mudhole and it took until three in the afternoon to get out of it. We went in a car to get some lumber to jack up the car until we could get going. I then hired another man who said he knew of a new road. He went twenty miles with us to a little town named Brawley, about ten miles from El Centro. . . . The next morning I hired a man to take us across the streams where there were no bridges."

There were no motels, or even tourist cabins, where motorists could sleep on a long trip. Small towns sometimes had hotels, but, failing that, the early automobile traveler just had to ask in town for a place to sleep, and take his chances.

"We stopped at a little hotel," said Edward Ayer, "with an old man and woman in charge, each striving to see which could look the dirtiest. I asked the woman if there was anyone to carry our baggage to the room."

" 'I haven't saw nobody to carry no baggage," she snipped.

"When I mentioned it to her husband, he said 'You don't have to stay if you don't like it,' and so we didn't. We drove seventeen miles farther and found a room almost bare of furniture. I asked the landlord where we should wash.

" 'Out at the creek running near the back door,' he said."

Camping and Exploring by Auto

Even camping looked enjoyable with an automobile. As soon as a family or group decided to go camping, someone was sent off to the local library with tracing paper to copy a map of where they wanted to go. Road maps were almost nonexistent.

The ideal camping party was made up of six or eight people traveling in two cars of the same make. That way if one car should break down, the parts from the other car could be pirated so that one car could be driven for help.

There was much to do to ready the auto for camping. The seats needed oilcloth covers to protect them in the rain and some sort of tarpaulin-covered roof on a frame, with side curtains to roll down, to shield the passengers as well as the car from bad weather. For a trip into rough country, the car needed a detachable piece of sheet iron attached to the bottom so rocks would not puncture its vital parts. The driver also had to pack a long rope, enough chain to go around four wheels, a jack, ax, shovel, and block and tackle.

Real campers were supposed to shoot or fish for their food, but many had to rely on "the tin can plan." Food and utensils for camping had to be packed in a large wicker basket. All food that was not in tins was packed in a wooden box. People who were used to taking glassware and china plates along on picnics had to learn that camping was different. Aluminum pans for cooking and eating for four persons cost $16. Campers bought a folding camp stove that collapsed into a small package. In the West, where there were larger logs to cook on, the camper used a zigzag iron frame. All cooking was done over a wood fire. The tiny alcohol lamp was only large enough to heat up water for one cup of tea. The true camper prided himself on cutting his own wood for cooking, not stealing it from a farmer's fence.

Wearing wrinkled clothes in the early 1900s was not refined —even at a campsite. People who cared sent their clothing in trunks by railroad to be picked up after they arrived at the campsite.

For bedding, the camper lined an oilcloth bag with a good warm horseblanket, closing up three sides to keep the breezes out. A "blow bed" of India rubber could be inflated with a tire pump. Otherwise a bag of ticking (mattress fabric) was filled with hay, straw, or leaves. In summer the men often slept in hammocks. The best tent was of waterproof silk with a floor-cloth. A camper took along a canvas "war bag" for the personal items, such as medicine and adhesive plasters.

As soon as the campers arrived at a site that seemed to have plenty of water and wood, the men took out the campstools. *Motor* magazine suggested that "a pair of folding campstools and a box of candy will help the womenfolk to maintain their composure while camp preparations are being made." If the little woman did not take kindly to camping, all was not lost. In 1902, an outdoorsman could buy a "portable automobile house" for as little as $75. The portable came in three sizes and could be put together in two hours. The most popular size was ten feet square, rising to nine feet high at the center. Already painted and shipped in sections, the house even had a door and two windows. These were the first summer cottages at many resort sites.

"Frontiering" where no automobile had ever been before added to the fun of automobile touring. It meant climbing mountain passes used by the pioneer and his mule, coasting down rocky roads that dropped off into picturesque chasms, scouting out paths used by the Indians and pony express riders, and cutting off across roadless plains.

W. W. Price and Philip Delany traveled nine hundred miles in nine days, dropping in on Pueblo Indians and surprising Mexican ranchers with their first sight of a gasoline-powered automobile. A tourist could follow their trail today, but this time on a road, by taking Route 64 out of Raton, New Mexico, circling through Taos and Santa Fe, then following Route 85 through Las Vegas, New Mexico, back to Raton. Some of the road, even today, is considered less than "super." Modern travelers, though, will find it hard to imagine what it was like in 1902, when the best part of the road was a cattle trail.

"From Raton we left the railroad lines which paralleled us,"

One tourist built himself a "recreational vehicle" (1920)

said Delany, "and pushed across the level plains where cattle turned and ran in herds at the sight of a motor on the old Mexican land grant."

After spending the night in an old adobe house in Cimarron, near where the Philmont Boy Scout Ranch is today, the adventurers entered a canyon.

"Its rocky walls echoed in hollow calls the throbbing of the machine," Delany continued. "As we hurried along, a fuzzy-coated burro walked out placidly before the car and nonchalantly jogged along in front of us."

They followed the burro into Elizabethtown, where thousands of gold miners had scrambled for dust in 1868. The only way out of the village surrounded by high mountains was through a pass that Delany said the Indians called "arrow stick in pole" (now Palo Flechado). From the summit of the pass, the car coasted down to the irrigated plain of Taos, watched by Indians and Mexicans resting on their hoes.

"Three miles beyond, we swooped suddenly down upon the settlement of five-story terraced houses of the Red Willow Indians. In their gaudy blankets they swarmed to the earthen housetops and watched us intently. After much coaxing, we crowded the car with redskins and dashed up and down at breakneck speed. There were such war whoops as city dwellers never hear."

The Indians who lived then in Pueblo de Taos invited the tourists to an underground council chamber to listen to the story of their faith in return for their first automobile ride.

Two proud drivers were the first to reach Crocker's Station on the way to "Yo Semite"

Today tourists can visit Pueblo de Taos during the daylight hours.

"They are a fine example of the early American aristocracy at its best," said Delany. "They have some lessons for modern American society, too."

After visiting the grave of Kit Carson in Taos, which tourists today can still see, the two men pushed several miles through sand to the cliff dwelling of "Pajorito Park," and then to Santa Fe. They passed wagonloads of Indians dressed in bright colors. The horses reared and jumped with fright until the auto was out of sight. The travelers stopped to fish along the road to Las Vegas, where the wild greenwoods were cut through with streams filled with trout.

The men enjoyed the stir they created going through the little village of San Jose, which looked as if it had not changed in a century.

"We went through the place like the wind, the machine snorting, whistle tooting, while the poor inhabitants huddled into frightened groups out of reach. We were a kind of first thunderstorm to them."

Coast to Coast

Nothing could prove that automobiles were here to stay so well as one transcontinental trip. Many people tried, like the Davises, but, for a long time, none of the easterners heading west made it to the coast.

Then one day in 1903, two westerners drove east. On May 23, Dr. H. Nelson Jackson and Sewall K. Crocker hopped into a 20-horsepower Winton touring car to win a fifty-dollar bet. They drove from San Francisco to New York in sixty-four days.

Jackson and Crocker packed the car with sleeping bags, clothing, a rifle, pistols, ammunition, tools, axes, a 20-gallon

Tom Fetch's 1903 Packard, *Old Pacific,* bogs down in Nebraska mud

auxiliary gasoline tank, and a block and tackle. That same Winton car is at the Smithsonian Institution today, minus the mud and dust picked up along the road.

Cowboys gave the men directions, often pointing them across fields that had never seen a path, let alone an auto. One memorable time, Crocker had to walk 29 miles to find gasoline. A sheepherder fed them one day when they had gone 36 hours without any food. Once they drove 25 miles with a broken axle. They had "fixed it," temporarily, by shoving the broken axle ends into a piece of pipe.

When they reached New York, the pair collected their fifty dollars, but Jackson figured the trip had cost him about eight thousand.

The fastest trip, coast to coast, was also from west to east the following year. E. T. Fetch drove M. C. Krarup, a writer, across a shorter route than Jackson and Crocker had taken, and reached New York one day earlier.

"We traveled in almost complete ignorance of what the next

Fetch stops for a rest on a superhighway in 1903

turn of the road would bring forth," said Krarup.

They headed out of California on the old stage road used by the forty-niners. They crossed ravines and dry washes, met roaming herds of cattle and horses that almost completely barred the way at times. They were careful crossing the Sierras to wait at way stations for stagecoaches, knowing the noisy gasoline motor might frighten the horses into a serious accident. Once in the Sierras, the car slid down a muddy descent of two miles in nine breathless minutes. The brakes were on the whole time. Often, climbing steep mountains, they had to stop to cool the brake rings.

"You'll never get through the sand hills of Nevada," said sheepherders. They were almost right. But Fetch had a trick up his sleeve for the sand. He had strips of canvas, six feet wide and 24 feet long. With these he laid out his own canvas road. It was very slow going, but it worked. The men forded shallow streams and even "jumped" out of some gullies. To "jump,"

Fetch set the motor at full speed. The car jerked upward ten or twelve feet, then Krarup quickly put chocks under the rear wheels so the car could not roll backward.

In Nebraska, snatches of very good road ended in mudholes. Following the old wagon train road at one point, the men came to huge rocks that wagons had been able to straddle. But the car wheels were much lower, so Krarup had to reroute the road over the rocks. Putting small stones in the ruts and building gradual rises up to the rocks, the men could make the wheels lift the car just enough to pass over the rocks. The men spent three hours traveling over just two miles of road this way.

A state highway in Colorado had been blasted out of solid rock and followed the stream, but the roadbed was such slippery and slimy clay that they had to put chains around the tires to move. While Fetch drove, Krarup walked beside the car, pushing it bodily away from the edge of the road which went off into sheer space.

Wirecutters turned out to be a handy driving tool when the pair were east of Denver. There cattlemen had fenced in large blocks of land with barbed wire without any regard to where the road was. Grasshoppers swarmed around when the car moved slowly, but when it was able to move faster, the insects hit them in the face, causing huge welts.

One night they came to a network of irrigation ditches and could not find their way out of the maze. Finally, at 4 A.M., they woke up a farmer who showed them the way out. From the town of North Platte to Columbus, Nebraska, the road was in water and mud the whole way. Seven times in one day they were stuck so fast they thought they would never get out. They reached "civilization"—meaning a real road—at Wheatland, Iowa. From there to New York the driving was beautiful in comparison.

The last night of the trip was a dry one. They picked up an escort to lead them into New York, because it was so dark.

"A wild night drive into the city," said Krarup. "We followed close upon the heels of a leader and, guided solely by his tailboard light, terminated the transcontinental trip in a cloud of dust—which is nearly always the penalty that the motorist pays for the civility of an escort."

As soon as a few adventurers had proven that automobiles actually could cross the United States, the future began to look bright for the "self-propelled" autos. One more giant step was needed before they took over the roads—and that was for someone to make a car that ordinary people could afford. That car, Henry Ford's Model T, was only a few years in the future. The Model T was not Ford's first car—but his 1908 model sold for only $850, and each year it was a little cheaper. At long last, traveling faster than a horse was available to almost everyone.

6
Old-Time Traveling Today

"All Aboard"

You can still feel the thunk of the steamboat paddle wheel, the sway of the trolley car, and the rattle of an antique automobile. You can turn back the calendar and discover for yourself why a train was called a "choo-choo" when your grandparents were small.

You may even hear the toots and tweets of the steam calliope that was first attached to a steamboat in 1856. This "steam pianna" was so effective in attracting crowds to the riverbank that showboats and floating circuses used it to announce their arrival. Today its raucous sound may be heard aboard the *Mississippi Queen* and the *Delta Queen* as they travel the Mississippi and Ohio rivers. You can travel on these stern-wheelers, sitting on a balcony outside your cabin, just as Charles Dickens did. You may even take part in the once-a-year Great Steamboat Race as the two rivals churn 1,500 miles up the Mississippi River to St. Louis with flags flying, Dixieland bands playing, and onlookers cheering from the shore.

Hundreds of steamboat, railroad, trolley, and auto museums all across America are just waiting for you to drop in. But you

The *Mississippi Queen,* with an automobile on its bow, steams along the Mississippi River today

probably like action. That's why the list below includes only a few of the sleepy sort of museums. Almost all of those listed are throbbing with life—with rides through pioneer villages and forests.

Although a few of the steamboats and train cars may be replicas, most are the real thing. Some carry you to sights you could never see from your automobile. Avoid disappointment by writing ahead for fares and hours of operation. You won't need to pack a duffel bag, because, unless otherwise noted, these are short trips.

All aboard—and have a good journey traveling faster than a horse.

United States

ALABAMA

Gadsden: Noccalula Falls Park. One-mile train ride to a pioneer village.

ALASKA

Fairbanks: Four-hour stern-wheeler excursion on the Chena and Tanana rivers, with commentary.

Skagway: Narrow-gage 1898 railroad ride through awesome scenery to Whitehorse, Yukon, 6½ hours.

ARIZONA

Old Tucson: Steam train and antique auto rides.

ARKANSAS

Morrilton: Museum of Automobiles includes Dudgeon's steam carriage.

CALIFORNIA

Barstow: Train ride at Calico Ghost Town.

Buena Park: Knott's Berry Farm. Steam railroad.

Fairfield: California Railway Museum. Antique trolley ride.

Felton: Steam train of 1880 on 6-mile trip through redwoods on Roaring Camp and Big Trees Narrow Gauge Railroad.

Fish Camp: Daily summer trips on Yosemite Mountain-Sugar Pine Railroad steam train.

Fort Bragg: California Western Railroad's *Skunk* travels 7½ hours uphill through redwoods and across Noyo River.

Los Angeles: Travel Town, northeast side of Griffith Park. Steam train.

Perris: Orange Empire Railway Museum. Train and streetcar rides.

Rio Vista: California Railway Museum. Trolley ride.

Sacramento: California State Railroad Museum. Simulated ride through history in railway car.

San Diego: Maritime Museum has 1904 steam yacht. Cruise harbor on stern-wheeler, *Bahia Belle.*

San Francisco: Cable Car Barn and Museum. Paddle-wheeler *Eureka* at floating museum, Hyde Street Pier.

Santa Catalina Island: Sunset dinner on historic side-wheeler and tour around island.

Santa Clara: Marriott's Great America. Steam train ride.

Sonora: Westside Logging Company has steam trains and rides in paddle-wheeler and antique autos.

South Lake Tahoe: Tahoe, Trout Creek, and Pacific Railroad steam trains.

Suisun City: California Railway Museum. Rides.

COLORADO

Antonito: All-day ride on coal-burning train along Cumbres and Toltec Scenic Railroad to Osier through spectacular scenery. At Osier, return or continue by New Mexico Express to Chama, New Mexico.

Central City: Colorado Central Narrow Gauge Railway follows 1878 roadbed to Black Hawk.

Cripple Creek: A 4-mile steam train ride to abandoned mines.

Durango: All-day steam train trip through rugged mountains to mining town of Silverton.

Georgetown: Steam locomotive to the Georgetown Loop and Lebanon Mine. Persons who cannot manage stairways board train at Silver Plume.

Manitou Springs: Colorado Car Museum displays antique autos in proper settings; no rides.

CONNECTICUT

East Haven: Branford Trolley Museum. Ninety trolleys; rides.

East Windsor: Connecticut Electric Railway Association; rides.

Essex: One-hour steam train ride through Connecticut River Valley connects with riverboat cruise.

Mystic: Mystic Seaport Museum. Early steamboat; no rides.

Warehouse Point: Trolley rides and old train cars.

DISTRICT OF COLUMBIA

Washington, D.C.: Smithsonian Institution. Complete exhibit of early travel; no rides.

FLORIDA

Fort Lauderdale: Paddlewheel Queen 2½-hour excursion or 3-hour dinner cruise on Intracoastal Waterway. Gold Coast Railroad near airport; rides.

Lake Buena Vista: Walt Disney World. Steamboat ride.

GEORGIA

Atlanta: Stone Mountain Park. Five-mile steam railroad trip; trolley ride.

HAWAII

Lahaina, Maui: Six-mile ride through sugarcane fields on old Lahaina-Kaanapali and Pacific Railroad.

ILLINOIS

Peoria: Stern-wheeler *Julia Belle Swain,* 1½-hour excursions on Illinois River.

Petersburg: A 45-minute cruise on Sangamon River in *Talisman,* a replica of 1832 steamboat.

Union: Illinois Railway Museum. Trolley and steam train rides.

INDIANA

Auburn: Auburn-Cord-Duesenberg Museum. Antique autos; no rides.

Indianapolis: Indy Hall of Fame Museum. Racing cars; no rides.

IOWA

Des Moines: Adventureland Park. Old trolley ride through Iowa of the 1890s.

Dubuque: Stern-wheeler, *Spirit of Dubuque,* 1½-hour ride.

Keokuk: Stern-wheeler, *George M. Verity,* river museum; no rides.

KENTUCKY

Cave City: Wondering Woods. Trolley through an 1890s village.

Louisville: A 2½-hour ride on the Ohio River aboard stern-wheeler *Belle of Louisville.* Kentucky Railway Museum. Steam train excursions.

Pleasant Hill: Paddle-wheeler *Dixie Belle* on the Kentucky River.

LOUISIANA

New Orleans: Stern-wheeler *Natchez,* 2-hour cruise of harbor.

MAINE

Boothbay Harbor: Boothbay Railway Museum Village. Train and antique auto rides.

Kennebunkport: Seashore Trolley Museum. A 2¼-mile trolley ride; dining car serves meals.

Rockland: Owl's Head Transportation Museum. Special events and working displays on weekends.

Wells: Wells Auto Museum. Many old cars; rides in 1911 Model T.

MARYLAND

Baltimore: B & O Railroad Museum, oldest in the country; no rides. Baltimore Street Car Museum. Trolley rides.

St. Michael's: Chesapeake Bay Maritime Museum. Bay boat collection; no rides.

Wheaton: National Capital Trolley Museum. A 2¼-mile trolley ride.

MASSACHUSETTS

Boston: Museum of Transportation. Steamboat rides.

South Carver: Edaville Railroad steam train, 5½ miles through cranberry bogs; horse trolley rides.

MICHIGAN

Dearborn: Greenfield Village and Henry Ford Museum. Paddle-wheel steamboat and 2½-mile steam train rides.

Flint: Genessee Recreation Area and Historical Crossroads Village. A 45-minute ride on Huckleberry Railroad.

Fraser: Michigan Transit Museum. Railroad and trolley rides.

Irish Hills: Stagecoach Stop, U.S.A. Train rides.

Marquette: Two-hour rides on Marquette and Huron Mountain Railroad, including one ride with breakfast.

Oscoda: Two paddle-wheel riverboats on Au Sable River, rides.

Saugatuck: Stern-wheeler *Queen of Saugatuck,* takes 1½-hour trip down Kalamazoo River to Lake Michigan.

Soo Junction: Toonerville Trolley ride and steamboat to the rapids of Tahquamenon River.

MINNESOTA

Brainerd: Lumbertown, U.S.A. Steam train and *Blue Berry Belle* riverboat rides.

Duluth: Lake Superior Museum of Transportation and Industry. No rides.

Minneapolis-St. Paul: 1½-hour trip around Fort Snelling on a stern-wheeler replica.

MISSOURI

Branson: Silver Dollar City. Steam railroad and an Ozark pioneer village.

Lake of the Ozarks: Paddle-wheeler *Tom Sawyer,* rides.

Glencoe: Wabash, Frisco, and Pacific Association Steam Railroad Museum. No rides.

MONTANA

Butte: Replica of early open streetcar tours city.

Virginia City: Nevada City. Rides on Alder Gulch Short Line.

NEBRASKA

Grand Island: Stuhr Museum of the Prairie Pioneer. Steam train ride and a re-created 1860s village.

Minden: Harold Warp Pioneer Village. Antique autos and steam train.

NEVADA

Virginia City: Virginia and Truckee Railroad to Gold Hill.

NEW HAMPSHIRE

North Conway: Eleven-mile train ride through Saco River Valley

North Woodstock: Clark's Trading Post. Old woodburner of White Mountain Central Railroad, rides.

Wolfeboro: Two-hour ride around lakes on Wolfeboro Railroad.

NEW JERSEY

Allaire: Pine Creek Railroad, rides around village and Howell iron forge.

Flemington: Black River and Western Railroad, 11-mile ride to Ringoes and back.

Newfoundland: Morris County Central Railroad, rides.

Morristown: Speedwell Village. Iron works and home of Alfred Vail, who built engine for *Savannah.* No rides.

NEW MEXICO

Chama: See Antonito, Colorado.

NEW YORK

Arcade: A 15-mile steam train ride on Arcade and Attica Railroad.

Mayville: Steam-powered stern-wheeler *Chautauqua Belle;* rides.

Rome: Steam train ride through old Erie Canal village.

West Henrietta: Steam train ride through historical scenes.

NORTH CAROLINA

Blowing Rock: Ride on Tweetsie Railroad.

Cherokee: Frontierland. Steam train ride.

NORTH DAKOTA

Fargo: Bonanzaville, U.S.A. Steam train and pioneer village; rides.

OHIO

Cincinnati: Home base of *Delta Queen* and *Mississippi Queen*, modern stern-wheelers.

Grand Rapids: Toledo, Lake Erie, and Western Railway's *Bluebird Special*, 2-hour ride to Waterville.

Marietta: Ohio River Museum. Old riverboats.

Nelsonville: Hocking Valley Scenic Railway's 1916 steam locomotive and 6-mile trip.

Worthington: Ohio Railway Museum. Trolley and train rides.

Zanesville: 1900 stern-wheeler *Lorena,* ride up Muskingum River.

OREGON

Cottage Grove: 35-mile steam train ride through a historic valley.

PENNSYLVANIA

New Hope: New Hope and Ivyland Railroad, 1911 steam train, ride 14 miles through Bucks County.

Orbisonia: East Broad Top Railroad, 10-mile trip.

Philadelphia: Franklin Institute, slowly moving steam locomotive. Steam warship U.S.S.*Olympia,* on waterfront; no rides.

Rockhill Furnace: Railways to Yesterday Museum; trolley rides.

Strasburg: Railroad Museum of Pennsylvania. Strasburg Railroad, 45-minute steam train rides.

Washington: Arden Trolley Museum; rides.

SOUTH DAKOTA

Deadwood: Ride into town by steam railroad.

Hill City: Two-hour steam train ride through Black Hills.

TENNESSEE

Chattanooga: Tennessee Valley Railroad and Museum, Inc. Steam train excursions.

Memphis: Mud Island. Unusual Mississippi riverboat museum. Replica of 1870 steamboat.

Nashville: Dual stern-wheeler *Belle Carol* steams on Cumberland River; rides.

TEXAS

Waco: Stern-wheeler *Brazos Queen,* 1¼-hour ride on Brazos River.

Wimberley: Steam train ride and pioneer town.

UTAH

Farmington: Lagoon Amusement Park; rides.

Promontory: Golden Spike National Historical Monument. Where the first transcontinental railroad was completed. Steam locomotives.

Heber City: Wasatch Mountain Railway's *Heber Creeper,* 3½-hour trip to Bridal Veil Falls past re-created frontier town.

Salt Lake City: Shoppers' mall built of trolleys, no rides.

VERMONT

Bellows Falls: Steam Town. Steam railroad rides.

VIRGINIA

Norfolk: Carrie B., replica of double-deck riverboat, tours harbor.

WASHINGTON

Park: Lake Whatcom Railway, 1½-hour steam train ride.

Snoqualmie: Puget Sound and Snoqualmie Valley Railroad, 5-mile steam train ride and trolley rides.

Tacoma: Washington Forest Products Museum, Point Defiance Park. Steam train ride through an old-time logging camp.

WEST VIRGINIA

Cass: 2- and 4½-hour steam train rides on Cheat Mountain.

WISCONSIN

Baraboo: Mid-Continent Railway Museum, 9-mile ride.

East Troy: Trolley museum, excursion rides.

Hayward: Historyland. Steamboat replica cruises river.

La Crosse: Double-deck paddle-wheeler *La Crosse Queen* on the Mississippi River.

Laona: Lumberjack Special, steam train ride to logging village.

Canada

ALBERTA

Calgary: Heritage Park. Stern-wheeler ride.

BRITISH COLUMBIA

Fort Steele: Locomotive rides through a Victorian village.

Vancouver: Steam engine *Royal Hudson,* 6-hour trips to Squamish.

MANITOBA

Winnipeg: Paddle-wheel riverboat rides on Red River.

ONTARIO

Ottawa: National Museum of Science and Technology. Steam train ride.

QUEBEC

St. Constant: Delson-St. Constant Canadian Railway Museum.

SASKATCHEWAN

Moose Jaw: Western Development Museum.

YUKON TERRITORY

Dawson City: S.S. *Keno* has Klondike tours.

Whitehorse: Stern-wheeler S.S. *Klondike* can be boarded. *See* Skagway, Alaska, for steam railroad ride to Whitehorse.

Picture Credits

The author is indebted to the following for photographs in this book:

American Automobile Association, p. 185
American Philosophical Society, pp. 10, 28
Automobile Girls at Newport, p. 155
Ballou's Pictorial Drawing-Room Companion, pp. 85, 125
Bancroft Library, University of California at Berkeley, p. 192
Delta Queen Steamboat Company, p. 199
Frank Leslie's Illustrated Newspaper, pp. 41, 66, 71, 87, 89, 103, 113, 126, 134, 151
Free Library of Philadelphia, Automobile Collection, pp. 194, 195
Harper's Bazaar, p. 132
Harper's New Monthly Magazine, p. 46
Harper's Weekly, pp. 33, 42–43, 54–55, 59, 106, 129
Harper's Weekly Supplement, p. 88
Illustrated London News, p. 79
Leslie's Weekly, p. 142
Our New West, pp. 100, 105
Smart Set Magazine, pp. 162, 166, 168
Stevens Institute of Technology, p. 109 (Painting attributed to Charles B. Lawrence)
U.S. Bureau of Public Roads, National Archives, p. 158
U.S. Department of Interior, National Park Service, pp. 184, 191
Harry Utzy, pp. 136, 138, 145, 164

Bibliography

Here are some of the books that helped me find out about traveling faster than a horse. Many are old and are found only in special libraries.

Alexander, Edwin P., *Iron Horses.* W. W. Norton & Co., 1941.

Beckmann, John, *Inventions and Discoveries.* Translated from the German, London, 1814.

Beebe, Lucius, and Clegg, Charles, *Hear the Train Blow.* E. P. Dutton & Co., 1952.

Bennett, E. D., ed., *American Journeys.* Convent Station, N.J.: Travel Vision, A division of General Drafting Co., 1975.

Bird, Isabella Lucy, *A Lady's Life in the Rocky Mountains.* Published 1879, republished University of Oklahoma Press, 1960.

Bowles, Samuel, *Our New West.* Hartford, Conn.: Hartford Publishing Co., 1869.

Bromwell, William, *Offhand Sketches, Companion for Tourists,* 1854.

Brown, Alexander Crosby, *Women and Children Last.* G. P. Putnam's Sons, 1961.

Bye, Ranulph, *The Vanishing Depot.* Livingston Publishing Co., 1974.

Copley, Josiah, *Kansas and the Country Beyond on the Line of the Union Pacific Railway.* J. B. Lippincott, 1867.

Crofutt's Transcontinental Tourist's Guide. New York: George A. Crofutt, 1872.

Dana, C. W., *Garden of the World, or The Great West (also Complete Guide to Emigrants).* Boston: Wentworth & Co., 1856.

Davison, Gideon M., *The Traveler's Guide Through the Middle & Northern States.* New York: G. M. Davison, 1840.

Dickens, Charles, *American Notes.* London, 1842.

Dohan, Mary Helen, *Mr. Roosevelt's Steamboat.* Dodd, Mead & Co., 1981.

Dwight, Theodore, *Sketches of Scenery and Manners in the U.S.,* 1829.

Emmerson, John C., Jr., compiler, *The Steam-boat Comes to Norfolk Harbor.* Portsmouth, Va., P.O. Box 112, 1947.

Emmerson, John C., Jr., compiler, *Steam Navigation in Virginia and Northeastern North Carolina Waters, 1826–1836* Portsmouth, Va., P.O. Box 112, 1950.

Fidler, Isaac, *Observations on Professions, Literature, Manners & Emigration in the United States & Canada, 1832.* New York: J. & J. Harper, 1833.

Floyd Clymer's Historical Motor Scrapbook: Model T Ford Edition. Clymer Publications, 1954.

Forbes, Robert B., *Remarks on Ocean Steam Navigation.* Boston Journal Office, 1855.

Fowler, John, *Journal of a Tour in the State of N.Y. in 1830.* London: Whittaker, Treacher & Arnot, 1831.

Hall, Edward H., *Appleton's Handbook of American Travel: The Northern Tour.* 9th ed. D. Appleton & Co., 1867.

Hamilton, Thomas, *Men and Manners in America.* Philadelphia: Carey, Lea & Blanchard, 1833.

Harper's New York and Erie Railroad Guide Book. Harper & Brothers, 1851.

Howland, S. A., *Steamboat Disasters and Railroad Accidents in U.S.* Worcester, Mass.:Dorr, Howland & Co., 1840.

Kane, Joseph N., *Famous First Facts.* 4th ed. H. W. Wilson Co., 1981.

Kemble, Frances Anne, *Journal of a Residence on a Georgian Plantation in 1838–1839.* Alfred A. Knopf, 1961.

Latrobe, J. H. B., *The First Steamboat Voyage on the Western Waters.* Baltimore: Printed by John Murphy, 1871.

Low, Betty Bright, "Women on the Move: Traveling 1800–1840." Ms. at American Philosophical Society.

Lyford, W. G., *The Western Address Directory.* Baltimore: Printed by Jos. Robinson, 1837.

McCullough, Joan. *First of All.* Holt, Rinehart & Winston, 1980.

Martineau, Harriet, *Society in America.* 2 vols. New York: Saunders & Otley, 1837.

Middleton, William D., *The Time of the Trolley.* Kalmbach Publishing Co., 1967.

National Railway Historical Society Bulletin, 10th Anniversary Ed., Vol. X, No. 2 (1945).

Northern Traveller, The. New York: Wilder & Campbell, 1825.

O'Gorman's Motor Pocket Book. E. P. Dutton & Co., 1903.

Philadelphia and Reading Railroad—Excursion Routes to Summer Resorts. Season of 1878.

Poesch, Jessie. *Titian Ramsay Peale, 1799–1885, and His Journals of the Wilkes Expedition.* American Philosophical Society, 1961.

Power, Tyrone, *Impressions of America 1833–35.* Philadelphia: Carey, Lea & Blanchard, 1836.

Prager, Frank D., ed., *The Autobiography of John Fitch.* American Philosophical Society, 1976.

Rhoads, W. W., *When the Railroad Came to Reading.* Newcomen Society of England, American Branch, 1948.

Ridgely-Nevitt, Cedric, *American Steamships on the Atlantic.* University of Delaware Press, 1981.

Silitch, Clarissa M., ed., *Mad and Magnificent Yankees.* Dublin, N.H.: Yankee, Inc. 1973.

Sketches of Scenery and Manners in the U.S. by author of The Northern Traveller. New York: A. T. Goodrich, 1829.

Smith, William P., *The Great Railway Celebration of 1857.* D. Appleton & Co., 1858.

Stein, Ralph, *The American Automobile.* Random House, n.d.

Stevens, Robert Livingston, Log of the *Phoenix,* 1809.

Stowe, Harriet B., *Palmetto Leaves.* Boston: James R. Osgood and Co., 1873.

Tanner, Henry S., *The American Traveler or Guide Through the U.S.,* 4th ed. Philadelphia: Published by author,1839.

Tasistro, Louis F., *Random Shots and Southern Breezes.* 2 vols. Harper & Brothers, 1842.

Thompson, Ray, *Willow Grove Park—A Look Back in Time.* Fort Washington, Pa.: Published by the author, 1979.

Trolley Wayfinder. Boston: John J. Lane, 1910.

Tunis, Edwin, *Oars, Sail, and Steam.* World Publishing Co., 1952.

Tyler, David B., *Steam Conquers the Atlantic.* D. Appleton-Century Co., 1939.

Wilson, W. Hasell, *Reminiscences of a Railroad Engineer.* Philadelphia: Railway World Publishing Co., 1896.

Wolf, Edwin, II, *Philadelphia: Portrait of an American City.* Stackpole Books, 1975.

I always like to check out newspapers and magazines, too, to see what people are saying about life in a particular time. Here are some of those sources:

Bulletin of the Historical Society of Montgomery County (Pa.), Vol. 17, No.4 (Spring 1971)
Early American Life, magazine, 1979
Electric Railway Journal, 1912
Everybody's Magazine, 1905
Frank Leslie's Illustrated Newspaper, 1895+
Godey's Lady's Book, magazine, 1861
Harper's Bazaar, magazine, 1901
Harper's New Monthly Magazine, 1852
Harper's Weekly, magazine, several years
Independent, The, magazine, 1901+
Journal of Franklin Institute, American Mechanics' Magazine, 1827
Ladies' Home Journal, magazine, 1903+
McClure's, magazine, 1901
Motor, magazine, 1905
New York Times, newspaper, 1899–1904
Norristown (Pa.) *Herald,* and *Norristown* (Pa.) *Free Press,* newspapers, 1833–1836
Outing, magazine, 1900–1908
Outlook, magazine, 1906
Philadelphia Bulletin, newspaper, 1968
Pittsburgh Mercury, newspaper, 1811–1842
San Francisco Chronicle, newspaper, 1915
Scientific American, magazine, 1894–1909
Spectator/Outlook, magazine, 1903
Woman's Home Companion, magazine, 1904
World's Work, magazine, 1903+

No history book would be complete without hearing from the people who lived then. Here are some of the people who helped me, without knowing it, by writing diaries, journals, and letters, so I could pass on their words and experiences to you.

Edward Ayer
John Boykin
Samuel Breck
Mary Donaldson
John Fitch
Robert Fulton
Jacob Harvey
Anna Howell
Benjamin Latrobe
Joseph LeConte
Charles Godfrey Leland
Dr. Samuel McCulloh
Louis McLane
George Nelson
Titian Ramsay Peale
Thomas Say
Ann Sellers
C.C. Sellers
George Sellers
Joseph Sills
Robert Smith
Robert L. Stevens
Jane and William Taylor
Annabel Williams

For places to go today for steam railroad, trolley, and antique automobile rides, I used the TourBooks of the American Automobile Association, which are published for its members.

Helpful libraries included:

American Philosophical Society, Philadelphia
The Atheneum, Philadelphia
Free Library of Philadelphia
Historical Society of Pennsylvania, Philadelphia
Library Company, Philadelphia
Maritime Museum Library, Philadelphia
Maryland Historical Society, Baltimore

Index

Italicized numbers indicate illustrations

About the Author

SUZANNE HILTON was born in Pittsburgh, Pennsylvania, but a family pattern of moving often into strange new neighborhoods started an inquisitiveness that has never been curbed. She attended nearly a dozen schools from California to Pennsylvania before attending Pennsylvania College for Women (now Chatham College) in Pittsburgh and graduating from Beaver College in Glenside, Pennsylvania.

During World War II, she used her knowledge of languages as a volunteer in the Foreign Inquiry Department of the American Red Cross. After the war, she married Warren M. Hilton, an industrial and insurance engineer and Lt. Colonel, U.S. Army Reserve. With their son, Bruce, and daughter, Diana, the Hiltons traveled thousands of miles camping and sailing.

A busy free-lance writer, Suzanne Hilton has written eleven books, ten of which have been Junior Literary Guild selections. She now lives in Jenkintown, Pennsylvania.